DECADES

Bob Dylan

in the 1980s

Don Klees

sonicbondpublishing.com

Sonicbond Publishing Limited
www.sonicbondpublishing.co.uk
Email: info@sonicbondpublishing.co.uk

First Published in the United Kingdom 2021
First Published in the United States 2021

British Library Cataloguing in Publication Data:
A Catalogue record for this book is available from the British Library

Copyright Don Klees 2021

ISBN 978-1-78952-157-3

Typeset in ITC Garamond & ITC Avant Garde
Printed and bound in England

Graphic design and typesetting: Full Moon Media

DECADES | Bob Dylan in the 1980s

Contents

Introduction: A Thousand Miles From Home

If there's a lost decade among Bob Dylan's 60 years of making music, consensus opinion inevitably points to the 1980s. This isn't without irony, considering that Dylan actually released more albums of original songs in this period than in any of the three following decades; but context is everything. The 1990s started with the less-than-classic *Under the Red Sky*, but two collections of cover songs and a well-received performance on *MTV Unplugged* were followed in 1997 by his most successful album since the 1970s: *Time Out of Mind*.

Beyond returning Dylan to the Top 10 and earning both rave reviews and multiple awards, *Time Out of Mind* signalled the start of his ongoing renaissance as a songwriter. His work since then might not equal the standard he set with the 1960s albums that first established his reputation, but it's a remarkable run of success for any artist. Coming from an artist who'd been written off multiple times in a single decade made it all the more astounding. Even the eight-year gap between his two most recent albums of original compositions – 2012's *Tempest*, and the 2020 release *Rough and Rowdy Ways*, couldn't diminish the esteem built up over this time.

By continuing to release challenging new music, Bob Dylan seems poised to have the last word on the classic rock generation – the loose cohort of still-active artists who were also making influential records at the same time that 'Like a Rolling Stone' made Dylan impossible to ignore. At the very least, he seems like the member of this group most likely to make the last major artistic statement. In the 1980s, however, he was just *one* of the many icons from the 1960s and 1970s whose current work lacked focus and left them disconnected from audiences in one way or another. This affected Dylan more than most of his contemporaries. Unlike Paul McCartney or The Rolling Stones, the singer didn't have a recent commercial success to bolster his perceived relevance for younger listeners, and the dynamic with his older fans was even more challenging. Many of them seemed content to applaud him simply for playing harmonica on stage; others were frustrated that his new records weren't *Highway 61 Revisited* revisited.

While the decade as a whole found him struggling creatively and commercially, Dylan rarely let the latter dictate his handling of the former in the recording studio. In a 1986 interview for *Rolling Stone* magazine, he reasoned that 'If the records I'm making only sell a certain amount anyway, then why should I take so long putting them together?'. These comments came after a pair of albums – *Infidels* and *Empire Burlesque* – where the singer consciously sought help from the generation that followed him in an effort to give his studio work a more polished sound; albums where the end results made clear that his own instincts and inclinations inevitably dictated what he shared with the public.

That interview also came shortly before Dylan began rehearsals with Tom Petty and the Heartbreakers for their dual True Confessions Tour: an endeavour that conveyed a somewhat different attitude than Dylan took in the studio. The tour, which played many of North America's largest concert venues, included several stadiums where they shared billing with The Grateful Dead. A year later, Dylan himself shared the stage with the Dead at a series of summer concerts. Though his subsequent recollections revealed conflicted feelings about these shows, from the outside, the decision to tour with bands much more popular than himself, pointed to a desire to maintain at least *some* level of cultural prominence (at least in the moment).

That's not meant to suggest a lack of musical kinship with those artists, especially Tom Petty. Despite very little collaborative material being released at the time, Petty proved to be integral in Dylan's eventual return to form. Supergroups rarely bolster the artistic reputations of their individual members, but The Traveling Wilburys – uniting him with George Harrison, Jeff Lynne, Roy Orbison and Petty – were a notable exception to the rule. The stature of those involved – representing multiple generations of rock music greats – was an obvious factor, but one of the key ingredients was a quality not typically associated with Dylan, at least in the 1980s: humor.

The irreverent approach comes through in their 1988 debut album's credits, where the five members are presented as members of the fictitious Wilbury family – a clan whose colorful history was recounted in liner notes written pseudonymously by Monty Python's Michael Palin. This streak of humor is most prominent in the songs written primarily by Dylan, such as the double-entendre-filled 'Dirty World'. Working with four of the few artists who could legitimately be considered his peers had the dual effect of pushing him creatively, and making his writing and singing looser. In the process, he regained a balance between spontaneity and craft that characterizes so much of his best work.

Dylan's next solo album was a far more reflective affair than the Traveling Wilburys, but displayed a comparable sense of creative renewal.

Oh Mercy rounded out his 1980s work with the most consistent song collection he'd released in years. If not a masterpiece on the level of some of his albums that came before and after – or conceived as anything more than a solid collection of songs – *Oh Mercy* was noteworthy as the first Bob Dylan album in a long time where neither fans nor critics felt the need to equivocate about its quality. Despite lacking the ambition of *Infidels*, the absence of overt misfires at least ensured it wouldn't get bogged down in debate about the song choices such as still surrounds the earlier album.

There's a tendency among aficionados to assess Dylan's albums based more on the recordings he didn't use than those he did. Between the artist's own tendency toward second-guessing himself, and the frustratingly uneven nature of his output (especially in the 1980s), this is understandable. However, while that view speaks to intense devotion, it also hints at an elitist gatekeeping approach, and often short-circuits substantive discussion of the merits of the albums as they are. Rather than getting stuck in these alternate universes – whose divergence from our reality pivots on which take of 'Blind Willie McTell' got included on *Infidels* – this book focuses on what Dylan actually saw fit to release. *The Bootleg Series* will factor in, but traditional bootlegs, not so much.

Bob Dylan's 1980s work may suffer in comparison to that of the decades before and after, however, one constant is that he made the records he wanted to at the time. In his memoir, *Chronicles: Volume One*, Dylan described feeling disconnected from his songs for much of this time. Nevertheless, even the most flawed among his albums contains something of lasting value, ranging from tender ballads and declarations of faith (sometimes in the same song) to narrative epics. This variety is highlighted by both the 2014 charity tribute album *Bob Dylan in The 80s: Volume One*, and the more recent stage musical *Girl From the North Country,* which incorporates several songs from the period, alongside more widely appreciated classics. 'The play had me crying at the end,' said Dylan when asked about the show in a 2020 interview with Douglas Brinkley. 'When the curtain came down, I was stunned. I really was. Too bad Broadway shut down, because I wanted to see it again.'

It's likely that watching *Girl From the North Country* was Bob Dylan's most significant engagement with his 1980s music in recent years as the singer rarely features this material in his concerts. On the Never Ending Tour, which began in 1988, his most commonly-played song from the era – that same year's single 'Silvio' – was last performed in 2004. In a series of concerts he played in the fall of 2019 – his last until the one-off streaming performance *Shadow Kingdom* in July of 2021 – the decade was represented solely by 1981's 'Lenny Bruce'. While other songs from these years have been played more often, Dylan's deeply-felt ode to the late stand-up comic still seems emblematic. It's a reminder that there was always more to his *born-again* period than many acknowledged at the time. To understand his work – not just from the 1980s but in general – it's necessary to treat that material as an essential part of the larger story, instead of an aberration. As much as anything, the material he's released from this time reflects the singer's journey to a place of equilibrium between his reputation as a singular talent and his own genuine devotion to a broader songwriting tradition.

Prologue: The Language That He Used

In the beginning, there was Robert Allen Zimmerman – born in Duluth, Minnesota on the 24th of May 1941 to Abram Zimmerman and Beatrice 'Beatty' Stone, whose own parents emigrated from Eastern Europe in the early-1900s. The future Bob Dylan had the outlines of a traditional upbringing among the town's Jewish community. This continued when the family – now including younger brother David (born in February 1946) – moved to Beatty's hometown of Hibbing when Bob was six years old after his father contracted polio. Founded as a mining town, the history of Hibbing was tied closely to that of America's industrial expansion and contraction in the 20th century.

Bob's interest in poetry and music preceded his May-1954 bar mitzvah. As a ten-year-old, he wrote Mother's Day and Father's Day poems for his parents, and soon dabbled in a variety of instruments. Meanwhile, radio broadcasts from far-off places expanded his musical horizons beyond what local station WMFG offered, introducing him to the Grand Ole Opry and artists like Hank Williams: nicknamed the 'Hillbilly Shakespeare'. After he started recording, Bob identified the writer and singer of 'I'm So Lonesome I Could Cry' as one of his key influences, telling biographer Robert Shelton in 1978: 'If it wasn't for Elvis and Hank Williams, I couldn't be doing what I do today.'

As a teenager, Bobby Zimmerman fell under the twin spells of rock & roll and women – both of which he's maintained complicated relationships with throughout his life. In his 1959 high-school yearbook, his stated ambition was, 'To join the band of Little Richard', and he recalled attending Buddy Holly's show in Duluth earlier that year, shortly before the 3 February plane crash that killed the 22-year-old singer.

Bobby played piano and sang for a number of bands in Hibbing, the most prominent being The Golden Chords. 'We were just the loudest band around,' Dylan told an interviewer for *The Duluth News-Tribune* in 1986. The group wrote this part of their approach into local legend with their February 1958 performance at Hibbing High School's Jacket Jamboree. During their performance of Danny and The Juniors' then-current hit, 'Rock and Roll Is Here To Stay', the combination of the band's volume and the singer's 'crazy' behavior led the school's principal to cut off their microphones. The singer's school friend John Bucklen (who later became a DJ) discussed the incident with one of Dylan's biographers:

I realize now, of course, that there was a young Bob Dylan in his very early form. He was a little bit ahead of everyone, but he didn't seem to mind. Because he had such a fantastic confidence in his talent, he didn't care. He just said: 'Here I am. Either you like it, or you don't. I know what I've got is great.'

That confidence didn't keep his bandmates from moving on to other groups, however – by this point, many of the elements most associated with the singer had begun to manifest. He'd started writing songs – the first being an ode to actress Brigitte Bardot – and developed a propensity for both a reckless personal life and mythmaking. The latter aspect makes pinning down details of his life before fame – including the adoption of his more famous name – suitably difficult. Based on his first brush with rock-and-roll life outside of Hibbing, that's probably how he preferred things.

After he graduated from high school, he spent part of that summer working at a diner and staying with relatives in North Dakota. At the time, regional band Bobby Vee and The Shadows were considering adding a piano player to expand their sound, and someone (possibly Vee's brother) recommended Dylan, who apparently asked that they use Elston Gunn as his stage name – one he'd previously used fronting his high-school group The Rock Boppers. After playing a couple of local shows, the group decided not to add a piano player full-time and parted ways with Dylan. The tale took on additional (if not accurate) dimensions when Bob returned to Hibbing, and the claims that he played on their record 'Suzie Baby' persisted after he began attending the University of Minnesota later that year.

Though probably disappointing at the time, Bobby Vee's rejection of Dylan was just as well, because his interest in blues and other American music was already taking him in a new direction. Visiting a black Minnesota DJ called Jim Dandy with John Bucklen exposed Dylan to older blues and R&B records, and the process of discovery continued after receiving a set of Lead Belly 78rpm records as a graduation present.

By the time he left for college in Minneapolis – much to his parents' relief – he was fully committed to folk music, and spent much more time immersed in the local music scene than his studies. In addition to playing on weekends at local coffeehouse the Ten O'Clock Scholar – where he supposedly settled on Dylan as the spelling of his stage name – the singer absorbed as much new music and as many new ideas as he could.

Among the most influential figures during his time in Minneapolis was Dave Whitaker. Well-traveled and politically-minded, Whitaker shared stories about meeting the beat writers in San Francisco and folk singers in Greenwich Village, and likely introduced Dylan to the book that cemented his future course.

First published in 1943, *Bound for Glory* presented Woody Guthrie's account of his travels throughout the United States and becoming politically and musically active during the Great Depression. The author's story and vagabond image captivated Dylan, who adopted a persona inspired by it. After learning that the degenerative nervous system condition Huntington's disease had confined Guthrie to a New Jersey hospital, Dylan made contact with the folk music icon and resolved to visit him in person. Dylan visited Guthrie frequently during his first year in New York City, and people in his circle recalled him playing songs for the older man.

Dylan's pilgrimages to Greystone Hospital in 1961 were made possible by his decision to drop out of the University of Minnesota and move to New York. Migrating to Greenwich Village put him at the heart of the folk scene, and he came to know many of its foremost practitioners. These included Pete Seeger, The Clancy Brothers, Dave Van Ronk, and especially Joan Baez. Baez preceded Dylan in fame, but his own acclaim eventually far exceeded hers: one of several factors that made their relationship complicated in the years ahead.

Future Dylan biographer Robert Shelton's effusive review in the *New York Times* in September 1961 coincided with Dylan signing his first record deal. Having been rejected by various folk-oriented record labels like Vanguard (who released Baez's albums), the singer got the attention of producer John Hammond Sr. at one of America's most prestigious labels: Columbia. Hammond, with his famed eye for talent, first encountered Dylan as a guest musician at another singer's session, and after a more formal audition, signed Dylan to an initial five-year contract.

Recorded in November 1961 and released in March the following year, Bob Dylan's self-titled debut included just two original compositions, including 'Song to Woody'. The remainder were folk and blues songs from various traditional and recent sources, such as Blind Lemon Jefferson's 'See That My Grave Is Kept Clean'. Aside from a review in industry magazine *Billboard* predicting that, 'When he finds his own style, (Dylan) could win a big following', the album was largely ignored, and its poor sales won the singer the nickname 'Hammond's folly' within Columbia.

His second album – 1963's *The Freewheelin' Bob Dylan* – released after legally changing his name to Bob Dylan, ensured that the disparaging nickname didn't last. Unlike its predecessor, the majority of songs were the singer's own, reflecting a greater interest in politics and his feelings about girlfriend Suze Rotolo. Many of these songs were written the previous year, including 'A Hard Rain's a-Gonna Fall' and 'Blowin' in the Wind.' The former song, which borrowed its structure and melody from the centuries-old ballad 'Lord Randall', featured lyrics that conjured atomic and biblical apocalypse, making the mix of the new and the traditional that persists in Dylan's work emblematic. The latter song became one of that body of work's defining moments. When recorded by Peter, Paul and Mary, it just missed the pinnacle of the US pop charts – kept from the top spot by Stevie Wonder, who had a hit with his own version of the song a few years later.

'Blowin' in the Wind' became an anthem for the civil rights movement, and was performed at the March on Washington in 1963, inspiring Sam Cooke to write an anthem of his own: 'A Change Is Gonna Come'. The song also represented Dylan's first major brush with accusations of plagiarism. Beyond any impact on his reputation, the significance lay in the money involved in publishing rights for a million-selling single. Aside from Dylan, the individual with the most at stake was his manager Albert Grossman, who received a portion of both his client's share and the publisher's, thanks to a behind-the-scenes deal with Witmark and Sons.

This allegation of plagiarism turned out to be unfounded, but also demonstrated something unavoidable for one of folk music's most active composers. Crafting new songs from the melody or other elements of existing ones was a long-accepted tradition among folk musicians. As with many traditions, the considerations changed once money was involved. 'The attempt to make sense out of copyright law reaches its limit in folk song,' said ethnomusicologist Charles Seeger (father of Pete). 'For here is the illustration par excellence of the Law of Plagiarism. The folk song is, by definition, and as far as we can tell, by reality, entirely a product of plagiarism.'

Repeating the claim of plagiarism for 'Blowin' in the Wind' wasn't the only thing that displeased Dylan about a November 1963 feature in the magazine *Newsweek*, especially considering the reporter's efforts to undercut his personal mythmaking. Nevertheless, the *Newsweek* piece was a turning point in his relationship with the press. Dylan's engagement with reporters became more antagonistic generally – not outwardly angry, but more likely to offer evasive or contradictory answers. Nevertheless, these exchanges still offered grains of truth, whether he intended it or not, like when he told Stuart Crump from university newspaper *The Brown Daily Herald*, 'Soon the new generation will rebel against me just like I rebelled against the older generation.'

Dylan's relationship with the folk music community also became more contentious as his notoriety grew. The singer's appearance at 1963's Newport Folk Festival – which featured his first public performance with Joan Baez, and previewed songs from his upcoming album *The Times They Are a-Changin'* – established him as a star performer in his own right, and not just a gifted songwriter. However, when he appeared at the 1964 festival, his songwriting had shifted away from the topical into a more personal direction, as heard on the August release *Another Side of Bob Dylan*. The disappointment of many within the folk community found its way into folk-oriented magazines such as *Broadside* and *Sing Out*. In *Broadside*, Paul Wolfe praised singer Phil Ochs' embrace of political music as Dylan put it aside as an example of 'idealistic principle vs. self-conscious egotism'. Irwin Silber, the editor of *Sing Out*, wrote an open letter to Dylan suggesting that his 1964 Newport performances showed that 'the paraphernalia of fame (was) getting in (his) way'. Silber added that on stage, he seemed 'to be relating to a handful of cronies behind the scenes now, rather than to the rest of us out front.'

Though he had the benefit of the community's criticism of Dylan, Phil Ochs was also among his most astute defenders. Ochs observed, 'It is as if the entire folk community was a huge biology class, and Bob was a rare prize frog. Professor Silber and student Wolfe appear to be quite annoyed that the frog keeps hopping in all different directions while they're trying to dissect him.'

The fault lines that existed after Dylan's 1964 performance were split wide open when he returned to the Newport Folk Festival in July 1965 accompanied by an electric rock band. Coming five days after the release of the 'Like a Rolling Stone' single, his performance of the song and two others elicited boos from the crowd. Among the folk music establishment, Pete Seeger's reaction – and his desire to cut the power cables – became the most iconic, but in keeping with most things Dylan-related, there was more to it. Seeger later clarified his position with the statement, 'I did say, 'If I had an axe, I'd cut the cable!' But they didn't understand me. I wanted to hear the words. I didn't mind him going electric.'

Equivocations from his peers notwithstanding, Dylan understood the divergence as well as anyone: 'Everybody knows that I'm not a folk singer,' he declared in a 1966 interview for *Playboy*. This led interviewer Nat Hentoff to reply, 'Some of your old fans would agree with you, and not in a complimentary vein.'

While he followed his electric performance at the 1965 Newport festival with acoustic renditions of 'Mr. Tambourine Man' and 'It's All Over Now, Baby Blue', and performed a full acoustic set prior to an electric one on his 1965-1966 world tour, the choice reflected *his* preference, not the audience's. He was aided in his efforts by one of the most enduring partnerships of his career; Canadian singer Ronnie Hawkins' backing group The Hawks supported Dylan on the world tour. After evolving into The Band, they collaborated regularly with him, both on stage and in the studio throughout the decade that followed, gaining artistic acclaim in their own right along the way.

In November 1965, Dylan took time out from his tour to marry Sara Lownds, the inspiration for numerous songs and mother of five of his children. In time, the singer would devote himself to family life, but in the short term, he was committed to more shows both in the United States and abroad.

A few weeks after the 1966 tour concluded at London's Royal Albert Hall, Dylan released *Blonde on Blonde:* the album many fans consider the high point of his 1960s work. He'd later describe the album – and its two predecessors *Bringing It All Back Home* and *Highway 61 Revisited* – as embodying the desired sound he heard in his mind. 'It's that thin, wild mercury sound. It's metallic and bright gold, with whatever that conjures up,' he told interviewer Ron Rosenbaum in 1978. 'We were doing it before anybody knew we would, or could. We didn't know what it was going to turn out to be.' Collectively, these three albums account for five of the singer's twelve Top-40 singles in the United States, and within his work are an era unto themselves.

The next one began with Dylan's nearly devastating motorcycle accident near his home in the New York town of Woodstock on 29 July 1966. Rather than go on tour again, he focused more on life with Sara and their children for several years; still recording but only playing live sporadically. One of these instances was a pair of January 1968 tribute concerts to Woody Guthrie (who had died on 3 October 1967) held at New York's Carnegie Hall. The star-studded lineup included Joan Baez, Judy Collins, Pete Seeger, and Guthrie's son Arlo. But Dylan's first live performance since the accident – once again backed by The Band – inevitably drew much of the attention.

The Band was also on hand for his performance at the Isle of Wight Festival on 31 August 1969. This show proved contentious, not just because Dylan played *there* rather than at the Woodstock festival held earlier that month (approximately 60 miles from the actual town of Woodstock), but also because his set started much later – and ended sooner – than the crowd expected.

Dylan remained musically productive during this time, recording with The Band dozens of songs that became known as the Basement Tapes by the time they were finally released years later, as well as numerous albums with other musicians. Some of these were better-received than others, but all of them were united by a more low-key approach than the trio of pre-accident albums. 1967's *John Wesley Harding* – which he later referred to as 'the first biblical rock album' – remains best-known in relation to Jimi Hendrix's rendition of its song 'All Along the Watchtower', while *Nashville Skyline* embraced country music, partially through a duet with Johnny Cash.

Aside from the experimental documentary *Eat the Document* – a follow-up of sorts to *Don't Look Back*, D. A. Pennebaker's portrait of Dylan's 1965 tour, Bob Dylan succeeded on his own terms in almost all respects in the 1960s. The 1970s were a far more complicated proposition. His stature ensured that new albums continued to sell well, but they still stood in the shadow of his older work. The 1970 double-album *Self Portrait* is arguably more famous from Greil Marcus' review of it – 'What is this shit?' – than any of its songs (many written by others), but the album still reached the Top Ten in several countries, and topped the British album charts. Even *Dylan* – Columbia's 1973 collection of outtakes released after a change in management led the singer to briefly move to Asylum Records – was certified Gold in the United States.

Planet Waves – Dylan's first album for Asylum – reunited him with The Band, and was timed to coincide with their joint 1974 tour. That tour and the accompanying live album, *Before the Flood*, were both popular, and further changes at Columbia facilitated a return to his original label.

Behind the scenes, his recent split with Albert Grossman would have future repercussions, but another potential split weighed on him far more heavily in the short term. After several years of living in Woodstock, Dylan and his family moved to California in 1973. Tensions in his marriage to Sara soon emerged, sparked by his return to touring and possibly an affair with a woman who worked at Columbia Records. Though the singer denies the stories of love gone wrong on 1975's *Blood on the Tracks* were autobiographical, the album – his first after returning to Columbia – inspired public speculation about the state of his personal life. Two contrasting reviews published in *Rolling Stone* are indicative of the initially mixed critical reception to the album, which is now firmly enshrined as one of Dylan's greatest – but the commercial success was undeniable.

The singer began working on his next album, *Desire*, showcasing two of the new pieces that would appear on it at the September 1975 taping of *The World of John Hammond*: a PBS tribute to the legendary producer (nearly a dozen years before his passing). Among the songs played for the special was 'Hurricane' – a song about boxer Rubin 'Hurricane' Carter, who many believed had been wrongfully convicted of a triple murder several years earlier. Released as a single, the song helped draw attention to Carter's plight, and the boxer was eventually released from prison after an intense legal effort.

The success of *Blood on the Tracks* and *Desire* (Both albums reached number 1 on the US charts and featured Top-40 singles) allowed Dylan to sidestep an emerging cultural force in music – the 1970s were full of *new Dylans*: Patti Smith and Bruce Springsteen being two of the more understandable recipients of the label.

The original Dylan, however, wasn't going anywhere except on tour. While hanging out with fellow musicians in Greenwich Village, the idea for what became the Rolling Thunder Revue, took hold. Beat poet Allen Ginsberg described the concept in an interview featured in filmmaker Martin Scorsese's 2019 movie about the tour:

> Sort of like a... con man, carny medicine show of old, where you just get in a bus and go from town – or a carriage, and go from town to town. It's like Dylan is taking us out to try and give us each... He's presenting us. I mean, that's his conception. I mean, it hadn't been made overt. His idea is, uh... to show how beautiful he is... by showing how beautiful we are... by showing how beautiful the ensemble is.

In addition to Ginsberg, that ensemble included guitarists Mick Ronson and T-Bone Burnett, violinist Scarlet Rivera, and singers Joan Baez, Renee Blakely, Ramblin' Jack Elliott, Roger McGuinn and Bob Neuwirth. The first leg of the tour ran for six weeks across the Northeast United States, emphasizing smaller venues, with the notable exception of Madison

Square Garden: site of the concert known as the Night of the Hurricane, on 8 December 1975. Another benefit show for Carter at Houston's Astrodome in January – with Stevie Wonder and Ringo Starr lending their support – preceded a further five weeks of concerts in April and May.

During the tour, the ensemble also worked on Dylan's quasi-narrative film *Renaldo and Clara*, which was eventually released in 1978 to largely negative reviews. Dylan and Sara portrayed the titular characters, while Ronnie Hawkins portrayed the Bob Dylan character. Other performers, such as Joni Mitchell and Roger McGuinn, appeared as themselves. Playwright Sam Shepard had been recruited as a screenwriter – however, since many sequences were improvised, he turned his attention to a journal about the tour (published as *Rolling Thunder Logbook*) and a role of his own in the movie.

The period between the final show of the Rolling Thunder Revue and the release of *Renaldo and Clara* was relatively quiet for Dylan. The live album *Hard Rain* sold modestly well, and he was one of many guest performers at The Band's farewell concert in San Francisco on Thanksgiving day 1976: documented in the 1978 Martin Scorsese film *The Last Waltz*. The most dramatic event came when Sara filed for divorce on 1 March 1977. The divorce was finalized in June, but a custody battle dragged on for many months. One of the conditions of the multi-million-dollar divorce settlement was that Sara wouldn't talk publicly about her marriage – in stark contrast to the accounts of relationships with the singer published by a variety of his later girlfriends.

With the 1970s winding down, Dylan found himself in a unique position as an artist. Other performers of his generation sold more records and concert tickets, but none of them had the same significance attached to their music. By the middle of the decade, the notion of Dylan as a poet – or, at least, a literary figure – had taken hold in academia, with college courses taught about his work, and Dylan scholars discussing it at the December-1975 meeting of the Modern Language Association. He was also being quoted by Presidential candidate Jimmy Carter, who he'd met during the 1974 tour with The Band when Carter was the Georgia governor.

The 1978 album *Street-Legal* and the world tour that followed received mixed reviews, ultimately leading Dylan into a space very few would've predicted of him. His life and career up to that point had encompassed numerous shifts in musical approach and personal narrative. As significant as many of those changes seemed in their moment, none compared to the development which dominated the following decade.

1980: A Door No Man Can Shut

'It would have been easier if I had become a Buddhist or a Scientologist, or if I had gone to Sing Sing,' Dylan mused in a May 1980 interview with journalist Karen Hughes for New Zealand newspaper *The Dominion*. The comment neatly summarized the singer's unusual position in the wake of his recent conversion to Christianity. Other artists had confounded their fans with major shifts in musical style – Dylan himself not the least of them – but his current expressions of religious devotion were perceived as a much starker break with his past work. And a much more difficult one for many to accept.

Hearing the man – whose first Top-40 single in the United States admonished listeners not to follow leaders – wholeheartedly embracing Christian dogma, clearly struck many listeners as being out of character at the time. However, what those who treat Dylan's overtly Christian albums as an anomaly often *miss*, is that the professions of faith they contained were no less passionate than the sentiments expressed in any of his 1960s landmarks or even *Blood on the Tracks*. For all that he's equivocated on spiritual matters since the early-1980s – and repeatedly (albeit erroneously) claimed not to have referred to himself as born-again – his convictions at the time appear to have been thoroughly sincere.

The period had its genesis in the tour promoting the album *Street-Legal*. After a concert in Arizona, 'Jesus put his hand on me', the singer told Hughes. 'It was a physical thing. I felt it. I felt it all over me. I felt my body tremble. The glory of the Lord knocked me down and picked me up.'

Dylan's reaction to the encounter prefigured an observation he made a decade later: 'People have a hard time accepting anything that overwhelms them.' Though the topic in that 1991 interview was more abstract, the mindset was something with which he had firsthand experience. In the wake of this encounter with the Almighty, Dylan initially found himself unsure of how to proceed and kept the matter largely to himself. He discussed it with very few people aside from background singer (and occasional songwriting partner) Helena Springs.

He began writing songs reflecting his newfound concerns, trying out a couple in December as his current tour was winding down, but apparently was reluctant to record them himself. In a 1980 interview, the singer told *Los Angeles Times* journalist Robert Hilburn that he'd initially planned to give the songs to Carolyn Dennis to sing, for an album where he might just produce. Dennis – who performed as a vocalist on several of Dylan's albums and tours in the 1980s – would have an exceedingly involved relationship with him over the next decade or so.

After some initial reticence, Dylan started a formal Bible-study course at the Vineyard Fellowship – a church in the Los Angeles neighborhood of Reseda – to which several members of his 1978 touring band already belonged. So did Dylan's girlfriend at the time – Mary Alice Artes – and some credit her with bringing him into the church's orbit, which also attracted Rolling Thunder Revue alumnus T Bone Burnett, and Hal Lindsey: author of the end-times bestseller *The Late Great Planet Earth*. As a practical matter, Lindsey's apocalyptic interpretations of biblical prophecies exerted far greater influence on the expression of Dylan's newfound faith than his former collaborator did, but some still believed that Burnett played a role in Dylan's embrace of the church.

Burnett has dismissed this notion on multiple occasions. 'I don't think one person ever converts another,' he told author Bill Flanagan in a 1984 interview for the book *Written in My Soul* – a collection of rock songwriter interviews whose subjects also included Dylan. More recently, the subject arose in a 2010 interview for *The Onion*'s *A.V. Club*. Discussing the move toward Christianity on the part of numerous musicians in the 1970s – a time in which the United States elected its first born-again President Jimmy Carter, Burnett commented: 'Probably about fifteen people out of that Rolling Thunder tour started going to church, or going back to church. I was implicated in that Dylan thing for a while. But no, there's no substance to that rumor.'

In any case, after several months of speculation, Vineyard Fellowship founder Kenn Gulliksen publicly confirmed Dylan's association with the church. In the May 1979 story from *The Washington Post*, Gulliksen shared the news of an upcoming album that would convey the singer's religious convictions 'in no uncertain terms.'

If Dylan's shift confused fans, at least a portion of his audience started out willing to give the new direction a chance. With an effusive review by *Rolling Stone* publisher Jann Wenner offsetting some of the more mixed assessments, 1979's *Slow Train Coming* – Dylan's first overtly religious album – became the singer's last Top-10 album in the United States until 1997's *Time Out of Mind*. 'Gotta Serve Somebody' – *Slow Train Coming*'s first single and his last Top-40 hit to date – also benefited from this initial goodwill as the new decade began. In February 1980, the song earned Dylan his first-ever Grammy award (his only one until a lifetime-achievement Grammy presented in 1991) for Best Rock Vocal Performance by a Male.

Shortly after the Karen Hughes interview, came the album that pushed many wavering fans off the fence. If the polished, accessible presentation of *Slow Train Coming* proffered an olive branch to Dylan's audience, the far more direct *Saved* was perceived by many as a sword. In the pre-internet era, an interview published in a New Zealand newspaper might not have been widely seen in the United States, but the album's content certainly wouldn't have surprised anyone who'd seen his recent concerts.

Membership in the Vineyard Fellowship carried with it a mandate to spread the gospel. For a figure like Bob Dylan, this meant not just recording albums, but performing publicly. Having decided to stop playing his pre-conversion songs in concert – in part, because he worried they were 'anti-God' – the singer needed more material. Fortunately, the enthusiasm for his newfound faith continued to inspire his songwriting. The majority of songs that ultimately appeared on *Saved,* debuted at the 1 November 1979 show that began a two-week stand at the Warfield Theater in San Francisco.

Despite the 1978 touring band's multiple connections to the Vineyard Fellowship, and an apparent desire to surround himself with fellow believers, the only veteran of that group included in the 1979 ensemble was singer Helena Springs. However, by January 1980, Carolyn Dennis had replaced Springs – suggesting a personal dimension to her falling-out with Dylan, who by all accounts remained devoutly reckless in his personal life.

Backstage drama aside, the band was defined by two key characteristics – in addition to having one of the more stable memberships of any of Dylan's touring groups up to that point, they displayed a peerless ability to convey the singer's message in concert. As with many great bands, the rhythm section provided the foundation. Drummer Jim Keltner was among the most in-demand session musicians of the 1970s and 1980s, with work on solo albums by all of the former Beatles (except Paul McCartney) being just one obvious highlight. Keltner – who also played on 'Knockin' on Heaven's Door' in 1973 – had declined previous invitations to tour with Dylan, but felt a profound connection with his new music. Bassist Tim Drummond played on *Slow Train Coming*, and though he was one of the band members who wasn't especially religious, he served as the tour's bandleader. Dylan offered some insight into his views about whether the almighty involved themselves in Earthly matters, by referring to the duo of Keltner and Drummond as 'the best rhythm section God ever invented.'

Guitarist Fred Tackett and keyboardists Spooner Oldham (whose credits included recording with Aretha Franklin and writing The Box Tops' 1968 hit 'Cry Like a Baby') and Terry Young rounded out the group along with the background singers. Despite being the musical element most associated with Dylan's religious music, he actually first incorporated background singers into his band for *Street-Legal* and the tour that followed. They were also the ensemble's most fluid component. On the initial leg of the tour, Helena Springs shared the stage with Regina McCrary (then using her married name Regina Havis) and Mona Lisa Young. Other singers would come and go even after Carolyn Dennis replaced Springs. The most prominent of these was Clydie King: formerly one of Ray Charles' Raelettes, and a recording artist in her own right.

The public reaction to the Warfield Theater shows is one of many areas of Dylan's life and career where fact and legend coexist uneasily. Reviewers for the city's main newspapers – *The San Francisco Chronicle* and *The San Francisco Examiner* – both offered dismissive assessments with their respective headlines 'Bob Dylan's God-Awful Gospel' and 'Born-Again Dylan Bombs'. *Chronicle* reviewer Joel Selvin described the material as 'some of the most banal, uninspired and inventionless songs of his career'. This prompted some readers to write to the *Chronicle* to ask if Selvin was deaf, but reports of fans booing and walking out of the show were echoed in other press outlets, often without context.

Rolling Stone was a notable exception. Their December story 'Dylan Tour Off to Shaky Start' acknowledged disappointed fans on opening night (some of whom asked for refunds), but added that audience response improved once the show's religious focus was understood. Famed concert promoter Bill Graham was another vocal defender of Dylan's new direction: 'I am deeply moved by what this man is doing. It's a very profound public display of personal convictions.' The magazine also reported that some within the tour had taken to referring to it as 'Newport revisited'. This reference to the mid-1960s uproar surrounding Dylan's decision to perform with a rock band at the Newport Folk Festival suggested a degree of self-awareness on the part of participants in relation to how polarizing the move to spiritual music would be among his fans.

That the issue this time around was the message more so than the medium, is ironic. Based on the recorded evidence, the band backing Dylan was as confident and capable as any in his career – traits shared by the singer himself in this period. When he brought them to Alabama's famous Muscle Shoals Sound Studio in February 1980 to record the follow-up to *Slow Train Coming* (also recorded there), the result should have been triumphant.

Saved (1980)

Personnel:
Bob Dylan: vocals, guitar, harmonica
Tim Drummond: bass
Jim Keltner: drums
Fred Tackett: guitar
Spooner Oldham: keyboards
Terry Young: keyboards, vocals
Clydie King, Regina McCrary, Mona Lisa Young: vocals
Barry Beckett: 'Special Guest Artist' (most likely keyboards)
Producers: Jerry Wexler, Barry Beckett
Engineer: Gregg Hamm
Release Date: US; 19 June 1980, UK; 20 June 1980
Chart places: US: 24, UK: 3
Running time: 42:39
All songs written by Bob Dylan, except where noted.

Side One: 1. 'A Satisfied Mind' (Red Hayes, Jack Rhodes) 2. 'Saved' (Bob Dylan, Tim Drummond) 3. 'Covenant Woman' 4. 'What Can I Do For You?' 5. 'Solid Rock'
Side Two: 1. 'Pressing On' 2. 'In the Garden' 3. 'Saving Grace' 4. 'Are You Ready?'

Detractors often characterize Bob Dylan's 1980s albums as exercises in squandered potential. There is some truth to that where *Saved* is concerned, albeit not for the reasons frequently cited. In principle, recording the album live in the studio during a break from the tour on which the same group of musicians had brought the songs to fruition on stage was an ideal approach. After an intense rehearsal and performance schedule, the group needed a break somewhere other than a recording studio, with a tight deadline for committing the songs to tape. A disconnect between Dylan and producers Jerry Wexler and Barry Beckett over how to approach the album's recording compounded the issue. Arthur Rosato – who worked with Dylan in various capacities in the late-

1970s and early-1980s (including being credited as 'Second in Command' for *Street-Legal*) – encapsulated the situation in an interview for Dylan biographer Clinton Heylin:

> You have a real famous producer and a guy who's never been produced, and they just didn't know how to work together. So what we did was go in the studio and record everything in a studio situation but live – but we just wanted to get out of there.

Considering how well *Slow Train Coming* turned out, Rosato was overstating the case that Dylan and the Muscle Shoals team didn't know how to work together. The primary issue seems to be that what the singer wanted musically, didn't mesh well with Wexler and Beckett's strengths. Where the previous album came together via a careful balance of meticulous craftsmanship and inspiration, the *Saved* songs had largely found their identity on stage already by the time the sessions started.

The raucous energy of the title track and other up-tempo numbers collided with the producers' efforts to replicate the polished feel of *Slow Train Coming*, ending up in a musical no-man's land. Jim Keltner – perhaps the band member most passionate about Dylan's new music – expressed particular regret that the album wasn't recorded in concert: 'It didn't want to be anything like *Slow Train Coming*. It wanted to have a big, open, live, exciting sound to match the praise (in) the songs. And it didn't happen. It didn't come across on the tape.'

Production is one of the least understood aspects of making an album, and the contrast between *Slow Train Coming* and *Saved* demonstrates something more mysterious. A producer can be ideal for one album but a poor choice for another: even a record from the same artist. The songs will usually have their own say in the matter. In the case of *Saved*, this means that, on balance, the slower songs are the most moving, but even among fans, this is poorly appreciated.

Saved remains highly resistant to reappraisal, and routinely ranks near the bottom of both fan and critic rankings of Dylan's work. Bearing in mind its status as the singer's first album to miss the US Top 20 since 1964's *Another Side of Bob Dylan*, it's fair to wonder to what extent this represents received opinion rather than genuine engagement with the music. The album performed better in the UK, but the question of whether fans judged these paeans to *the Good Book* by the cover, remains an open one.

British artist Tony Wright created striking album covers for artists ranging from Marianne Faithfull and Ramones to Bob Marley and Chic. The cover for *Saved* also fits that category but doubtless was off-putting to many potential buyers. Based on Dylan's description of a vision he had of Jesus reaching out to the faithful, it made the cross imagery used on the *Slow Train Coming* cover look like a model of restraint, and seemingly signaled another onslaught resembling preaching. In reality, *Saved* was the less preachy and judgmental of the two records. T Bone Burnett gracefully summarized the possible paths Christian songwriters can take when writing about their faith: 'If you believe Jesus is the light of the world, there are two kinds of songs you can write – you can write songs about the light, or about what you see by the light.'

Slow Train Coming tended to project outward about the state of the world, and present conventional wisdom on the perils of unbelief. Where it emphasized 'the light', *Saved* focused more on Dylan's personal perspective on his faith. The songs display a degree of humility not typically associated with such an iconic artist. The insistence on his vision for the album cover might be the one aspect of the album where the singer's ego got in the way of communicating his message. After radio stations were shipped the album in a plain white sleeve, Columbia Records ultimately traded Wright's painting for a picture of Dylan in concert, but the album's critical and commercial fate was already sealed, regardless of the quality of the music.

Saved opens with 'A Satisfied Mind'. The oft-covered song's many interpreters include three artists in Bob Dylan's orbit: Joan Baez, The Byrds and Johnny Cash. Dylan himself had previously recorded it with The Band during the *Basement Tapes* sessions, though that rendition wouldn't get an official release until a *Bootleg Series* edition three decades later. The 1980 studio recording came about almost randomly, as a single take between a pair of Dylan compositions. In different circumstances, opening one of his albums this way would've felt incongruous, but it made sense here. Philosophically speaking, it's a short walk from 'It's so hard to find one rich man in ten with a satisfied mind' to the 'Gospel of Matthew' and Jesus' admonition that 'It is easier for a camel to go through the eye of a needle, than for a rich man to enter into the kingdom of God.'

The album's title track includes something relatively rare for one of Dylan's songs – a co-writing credit for one of his band members: bassist Tim Drummond. While the studio version of 'Saved' lacks some of the immediacy of concert performances from this period, it makes its case forcefully nonetheless. The opening lyric's allusion to original sin – 'I was blinded by the devil, born already ruined' – quickly establishes the song's center of gravity. At the same time, this gospel-infused rave-up conveys a palpable sense of joy. Rather than seeking to castigate others, references within it to 'the pit' and 'the fire' are framed in the context of personal salvation and gratitude. One of the song's later lines talks about being spared 'Not by works, but by faith in him who called'. This reflects not only Dylan's own experience, but also the concept of *sola fide*: the belief commonly held in Protestant denominations, that man is not saved through good works alone.

Saved is followed by a pair of ballads, the slower tempos of which by no means indicate lack of commitment. 'Covenant Woman' demonstrates that Dylan's focus on the kingdom of heaven didn't preclude involvement in earthly matters, especially where women were concerned.

> You know we are strangers in a land we're passing through
> I'll always be right by your side
> I've got a covenant too

Several biographers have speculated about the identity of the woman to whom the singer desires 'to stay closer than any friend'. It's risky to conflate coincidence and causality where Dylan is concerned, but also worth noting that the song stopped appearing regularly in his setlists just a month or so after Helena Springs' departure.

'What Can I Do For You?' makes an effective companion piece to 'I Believe in You' from *Slow Train Coming*. In both songs, music and lyrics combine to create a powerful sense of spiritual conviction. Whatever trials life presents are offset by the power of his faith.

> And I walk out on my own
> A thousand miles from home
> But I don't feel alone
> 'Cause I believe in you

This stanza from the earlier song is just a different set of steps on the same path as...

> I know all about poison
> I know all about fiery darts

I don't care how rough the road is
Show me where it starts
Whatever pleases you
Tell it to my heart
Well, I don't deserve it
But I sure did make it through

Though Dylan's religious music made very few friends in mainstream circles, 'What Can I Do for You?' found support from a surprising source – Debby Boone recorded it for her own Christian album *With My Song*, which entered *Billboard*'s Inspirational LPs chart the same week as *Saved*. At the following year's Grammy Awards, Boone's album won the award for Best Inspirational Performance: beating out *Saved*, as well as records by Commodores and Willie Nelson.

The first side of Saved closed with another up-tempo song: 'Solid Rock.' Initially known by the title 'Hanging On to a Solid Rock', the more concise name better fits the song's insistent rhythm. While the subject matter's theological spirit is obvious in the lyric, there's an underlying message of perseverance and endurance. That may be a factor in Dylan's decision to play it in concert as recently as 2002. Most *Saved* songs haven't been performed live since the conclusion of the singer's late-1981 tour, but he apparently retained some sense of connection to this one.

In contrast, the song that opened side two was among the earliest of the overtly religious compositions to disappear completely from his setlists. Despite being one of this period's more powerful songs – both in concert and on record – the last live performance of 'Pressing On' came in May 1980 at the final show of Dylan's spring tour. Anyone looking for signs that his evangelical fervor had diminished, could use his decision to step back from such an overt profession of faith, to support their view.

However, the persistence of the album's next song tells a different story. Like 'Solid Rock', 'In the Garden' also made it to some of the Never Ending Tour's 21st-century performances. This powerful piece also figured in multiple tours across the 1980s and 1990s, including 1986's True Confessions Tour with Tom Petty and The Heartbreakers. Dylan's impassioned retelling of biblical accounts of Christ's betrayal in the Garden of Gethsemane and his later resurrection – with its echoes of the spiritual 'Were You There' – is noteworthy as his only song from the *born-again* period to use that phrase.

Nicodemus came at night so he wouldn't be seen by men
Saying, 'Master, tell me why a man must be born again'

The song featured in *Hard To Handle* – the HBO special filmed during the Australian portion of the tour. Though it was actually played rather late in the concerts from which the program was drawn, the film used it as the opening number: Dylan introducing it as a song about his hero. Putting aside the ambiguity this gesture fostered about Dylan's religious leanings as the decade progressed, it isn't surprising that the song itself continued to engage him. Comments made to journalist Cameron Crowe in the liner notes to the 1985 compilation *Biograph*, indicate that Dylan saw the piece as something unique in his work:

'In the Garden' is actually a classical piece. I don't know how in the world I wrote it, but I was playing at the piano, closed my eyes, and the chords just came to me. I can hear it being played by symphony orchestra or a chamber choir or something.

'Saving Grace' also went the distance to reach Dylan's 21st-century repertoire. The most recently played song from *Saved*, its most recent performance came at a 2012 concert in Pennsylvania, shortly before the release of the album *Tempest*. Sandwiched between songs from 2001 and 2009, this rendition wasn't especially revelatory, but the song's balancing act between the singer's longstanding interests in morality and mortality made it a fitting addition to a latter-day setlist.

By this time I'd-a thought I would be sleeping
In a pine box for all eternity

The song portrays Dylan's sense of personal salvation in more stark terms than anything else on *Saved*, except for the title track. It also finds him asking for forgiveness, though the intended audience for this plea is unclear. Elsewhere on the album, it's easy to tell whether references to 'you' are directed to the early or the divine, but the distinction blurs here.
'Are You Ready?' – the album's finale and the last song written for the record – displays no such ambiguity. More akin to 'When He Returns' and 'When You Gonna Wake Up?' from *Slow Train Coming*, it's a lyrical outlier on *Saved* in its willingness to challenge listeners about their faith. While posing a stark choice between heaven and hell, and with a reference

to Armageddon that superficially conforms to the popular perception of Dylan constantly haranguing his audience about Jesus, the song's construction argues against that reductive view. Midway through the song, he turns the underlying question on himself by shifting into first-person for the second verse.

> Am I ready to lay down my life for the brethren
> And to take up my cross?
> Have I surrendered to the will of God
> Or am I still acting like the boss?

Dylan returns his attention to the worldly 'you' in subsequent verses, but nevertheless remains engaged in the dialogue to the end. His final words on the album are, 'I hope you're ready.'

After leaving Muscle Shoals, the band returned to Los Angeles to perform at the Grammy Awards, playing 'Gotta Serve Somebody' the same night Dylan won his award for the song. The ensemble then took several weeks off – during which time *Slow Train Coming* received a Dove Award from the Gospel Music Association – before resuming the tour in April. The five-week run started in Toronto and Montreal before heading to the Northeastern United States. In Toronto, he introduced the provocatively-titled song 'Ain't Gonna Go to Hell for Anybody' – a fitting musical companion to his Hal-Lindsey-inspired onstage comments, which had not mellowed since the previous tour:

> Now we've had, you know, a lot of previews of what the Antichrist could be like. We had that Jim Jones, he's like a preview. We had Adolf Hitler... with a preview. Anyway, the Antichrist is going to be a little bit... a little bit different than that. Evidently, he's going to bring peace to the world for... for a certain length of time. But he will eventually... uh... be defeated too. Supernaturally defeated. God will intervene. But you're still gonna have to be aware of these things. You need something strong to hang on to.

The singer had apparently intended for these shows to precede a summer tour. Unfortunately, a record-setting US heatwave curtailed those plans, leaving a 21 May concert in Dayton, Ohio as the final live performance prior to the June release of *Saved*.

Dylan used this unplanned break to work on more new songs. He recorded versions of several with his band at Rundown Studios – the

Santa Monica building the singer had turned into a recording studio and rehearsal space at the end of 1977 – and performed others live during a brief tour that started in November. Many of these songs – such as 'Yonder Comes Sin' and 'City of Gold' – were unreleased outside of *Biograph* and various volumes from *The Bootleg Series*. One of them – 'Let's Keep It Between Us' – was later recorded by Bonnie Raitt. Only a handful of the compositions from this period ultimately appeared on Dylan's next album *Shot of Love*.

Among the songs not included on *Shot of Love* – at least on its original release – are a pair of compositions widely regarded as Dylan landmarks. Both 'Caribbean Wind' and 'The Groom's Still Waiting at the Altar' were performed live when the band returned to the Warfield Theatre in autumn. 'The Groom's Still Waiting at the Altar' made its concert debut on 13 November 1980, with Carlos Santana joining the band for the song. Performances at the next two San Francisco shows also featured guest guitarists Mike Bloomfield and Jerry Garcia respectively.

For all its acclaim among Dylan fans, the 12 November show remains the lone concert appearance of 'Caribbean Wind'. This happened at the request of Paul Williams – founder of the rock music journal *Crawdaddy*, and author of *Dylan – What Happened?*: a thoughtful volume about the 1979 shows at The Warfield. In a follow-up piece focused on the 1980 San Francisco shows, Williams observed frustration on Dylan's part about the band not following his lead on the song, but comments the singer made several years later point to other issues with the composition.

While neither of these songs were played live after November 1980, that month's concerts were more noteworthy for the presence of more familiar compositions. For the first time in nearly two years, Dylan performed material that preceded *Slow Train Coming*. When Robert Hilburn asked Dylan that month about the decision to revisit older songs, he talked about having felt out of touch with his older work on the previous tour: 'It's like I said, this show evolved out of that last tour. It's like the songs aren't... how can I put it? Those songs weren't anti-God at all. I wasn't sure about that for a while.'

The first of the November shows were promoted as a retrospective of Dylan's work, and only included five of his own older songs, plus Dion's 1968 folk-rock hit 'Abraham, Martin and John'. Based in part on Bill Graham's urging, the balance between older songs and the overtly religious work evened out considerably as the brief tour progressed. After starting 1980 with 'Pressing On' as a concerts finale, the year's final show concluded with 'A Hard Rain's a-Gonna Fall', suggesting a redirection, rather than abandonment of biblical zeal.

Shortly after that 4 December concert, Bob Dylan joined much of the world and many of his rock music contemporaries in grieving the death of John Lennon. Lennon's 8 December murder by fanatical fan Mark David Chapman profoundly impacted Dylan, who had attracted his own share of disturbed fans over the years. Fortunately, the fear of attacks on other 1960s rock stars that the singer related to his friend and future musical collaborator Ted Perlman, proved to be unfounded, and Dylan ended the year continuing to refine the craft for which he remains best-known: songwriting.

1981: The Warnin' That Was Before the Flood

One factor that's often overlooked when discussing Bob Dylan's born-again period, is that the self-righteousness detractors decried in his religious work had been there all along. The path from 'Masters of War' and 'Ballad of a Thin Man' to 'When You Gonna Wake Up?' might've been a winding road, but it wasn't hard to follow. Nevertheless, the fans and critics who enjoyed his lyrical evisceration of 'Mister Jones', or his equating the military-industrial complex with Judas, found such attitudes harder to appreciate when directed at themselves. The combination of scathing reviews and declining record sales suggested that many of these listeners took the sentiments of his newer songs personally.

No one but Dylan himself actually knows to what extent those reactions factored into the November-1980 decision to resume playing older songs or diversify the subject matter of his newest compositions. Paul Williams interpreted the previous autumn's shows as 'Clearing up some unfinished business', but Dylan himself offered little insight. Interviewers who ventured into these topics during his summer 1981 tour generally received confounding responses like 'I'm different, the songs are the same' or 'You kind of have to decide that for yourself'. Perhaps the most illuminating comment came when the well-known New York City DJ Dave Herman turned a July-1981 interview to discussion of the soon-to-be-released album *Shot of Love*. The singer responded with laughter: 'You don't wanna talk about *Saved*? No one wants to talk about *Saved*!'

Whatever he felt about his past work, Dylan began 1981 looking ahead to his 21st studio album – an impressive milestone unmatched by any of his 1960s contemporaries who were still active and recording new music. The detente he established between his older work and the current songs of praise, found a counterpart in his approach to producing the new record. Though he spent a great deal of time with his band refining the songs that comprised *Saved*, the recording itself had been something of a rush job that didn't fully reflect the inspirational spark present in their live performances. The path ahead for his latest songs involved both a statement of purpose and a certain degree of compromise.

The singer wanted a greater say in the album production, but also recognized the need for someone to help him actually get the songs recorded effectively. In late March, after a few weeks at Rundown Studios working on various songs, the band began what Arthur Rosato termed 'a studio tour' of Los Angeles, to find both the right person and place.

According to Rosato and members of the band interviewed by Clinton Heylin, locations ranged from studios set up in people's garages, to famous facilities such as United Western Recorders where The Beach Boys and Frank Sinatra recorded some of their most acclaimed work. Jim Keltner characterized the process as 'looking for a vibe', while Fred Tackett described Dylan's focus on finding people to work with 'who knew how to record old-style.'

Dylan's plans were put to the test on the most infamous excursion of this 'studio tour', which involved one of his most famous outtakes. While he only performed 'Caribbean Wind' once in concert, he recorded the song multiple times in different studios, including a 31 March session at Studio 55 in Los Angeles with producer Jimmy Iovine. Having worked as an engineer on albums by John Lennon and Bruce Springsteen in the mid-1970s, Iovine started producing records himself later in the decade – including Patti Smith's *Easter* and Tom Petty and The Heartbreakers breakthrough album *Damn the Torpedoes*. Despite this seemingly complementary musical background, the results of the session did not please Dylan, who revisited the song at Rundown a week later.

In fairness to Iovine, it's unlikely that any recording of 'Caribbean Wind' would've satisfied the singer, who'd been struggling with the song for several months. 'The song was fantastic to play', recalled Jim Keltner. 'But every time you'd hear it back, there was something missing.' Though Dylan clearly felt a connection with the song, the effort to find the seemingly missing piece ultimately collided with his songwriting approach: 'Sometimes you'll write something to be very inspired, and you won't quite finish it for one reason or another,' he told Cameron Crowe for the liner notes to the 1985 box-set *Biograph*. 'Then you'll go back and try and pick it up, and the inspiration is just gone. Either you get it all, and you leave a few little pieces to fill in, or you're always trying to finish it off.' Dylan's March 1985 interview with Bill Flanagan for the book *Written in My Soul*, echoed this sentiment:

> I don't have any expectations if I'm putting something down, that it'll be something great if I only get back to it. I keep it in front of me for a while, and if I don't have it done by a certain time... I'll go back and it'll still be there, but I won't be able to relate to it.

Just as these comments help explain many of the beloved songs Dylan left off his albums over the years, 'Caribbean Wind''s origins in 'Thinking about living with somebody for all the wrong reasons' (while sailing the Caribbean in his recently-built boat The Water Pearl) pointed to a shift in his preoccupations. Amid all the evocative turns-of-phrase in the available recordings, none seems more apt than 'the furnace of desire'. The end-times sensibility is still present, but balanced against more earthly concerns. While ultimately left off *Shot of Love*, this song – more than any other from the time – pointed to the overall direction the album would take.

Even at his most outwardly devout, Dylan's messy personal life clearly made an impact on his artistic decisions, if only in regard to the concert setlists. 'Caribbean Wind' revealed an inclination to be more honest about this thought process; at least, as honest as an artist known for pervasive evasiveness could be. Wrestling with these dueling impulses made *Shot of Love* a more dynamic piece of work than its predecessor, but also a more fragmented one.

Shot of Love (1981)

Personnel:
Bob Dylan – vocals, guitar, piano, harmonica and percussion
Clydie King – vocals
Jim Keltner – drums
Tim Drummond – bass
Fred Tackett – guitar
Regina McCrary, Carolyn Dennis and Madelyn Quebec – backing vocals
Additional personnel:
Danny Kortchmar – guitar on 'Shot of Love' and others
Steve Ripley – guitar on 'Shot of Love' and others
Carl Pickhardt – piano on 'Every Grain of Sand' and others
Benmont Tench – keyboards on 'Every Grain of Sand' and others
Steve Douglas – saxophone ('Every Grain of Sand,' 'Dead Man, Dead Man')
WM 'Smitty' Smith – organ ('Heart of Mine')
Ringo Starr – tom tom ('Heart of Mine')
Donald 'Duck' Dunn – bass ('Heart of Mine')
Ron Wood – guitar ('Heart of Mine')
Producers – Bob Dylan and Chuck Plotkin; Bumps Blackwell ('Shot of Love')
Engineer – Toby Scott
Release date: 12 August 1981
Chart places – US: 33, UK: 6
Running Time – 44:27
All songs written by Bob Dylan.

Side One: 1. 'Shot of Love' 2. 'Heart of Mine' 3. 'Property of Jesus' 4. 'Lenny Bruce' 5. 'Watered-Down Love'
Side Two: 1. 'The Groom's Still Waiting at the Altar' 2. 'Dead Man, Dead Man' 3. 'In The Summertime' 4. 'Trouble' 5. 'Every Grain of Sand'

Shot of Love's title song was the first one committed to tape in a manner Dylan found satisfactory, thanks to a late-April recording session overseen by veteran producer Robert 'Bumps' Blackwell. His resume included songwriting and production for several artists whose work crossed between the sacred and the secular; most prominently, Little Richard and Sam Cooke. Clearly not one to create genre-based barriers in music, Blackwell's obituary in the *Los Angeles Times* included the quote, 'It dawned on me when I was working with The Soul Stirrers, that all you had to do was replace 'Jesus' with 'baby' or 'darling''. That may help explain why Dylan clicked with him in a way that eluded other producers. Blackwell's 1960's work with Clydie King – Dylan's close confidant in music and other matters at the time – probably played a part also.

In the liner notes for *Biograph*, Dylan described Blackwell as having 'the best instincts' of any producer he'd worked with, and said that he'd wanted to record the whole album with him. Though various concerns – including Blackwell's own health issues – precluded doing so, another option soon presented itself: former Asylum Records A&R executive Chuck Plotkin. In 1976, Plotkin produced one of the decade's most ubiquitous pop hits – 'Still the One' by pop/rock band Orleans – and in 1978 began a long-standing association with Bruce Springsteen. Accounts vary on who suggested Plotkin to Dylan, but regardless of the backstory, Plotkin oversaw the recording sessions that yielded the remainder of the album.

In the 2008 documentary *Bob Dylan: Under Review 1978-1989* (aka *Both Ends of the Rainbow*), Plotkin recalled that, rather than focusing on the specific goal of making an album, he simply invited Dylan to come to his Hollywood studio and see what happened. The sessions at Clover Studios took place from the end of April into mid-May. In the studio, guest musicians – such as session guitarist Danny Kortchmar and keyboardist Benmont Tench from Tom Petty and The Heartbreakers – supplemented Dylan's regular band. In the ultimate sign of the informal approach to the recording, Dylan reputedly missed the first-scheduled session because he was in Minnesota, requiring the producer to give the frustrated musicians a pep talk.

Beyond the opportunity to work with such a legendary figure, Plotkin spoke of being motivated by the quality of Dylan's new material, which he saw as balancing the singer's religious convictions with the 'wild personal poetry' of his earlier work. The producer's most remarkable contribution was striking an effective balance between patience with Dylan's sometimes chaotic working habits, and the urgency of capturing good performances of the new songs before the singer got bored with them. This required Plotkin and engineer Toby Scott – who worked together on some Springsteen albums – to be pragmatic and opportunistic. In the *Under Review* documentary, Scott noted that they always started recording whenever 'Bob was in the room with his guitar on and anywhere near a microphone', to ensure that no performances were missed. Dylan decided to re-record several seemingly finished songs late in the sessions. Likewise, when Ringo Starr and Ron Wood visited Clover after the main recording had wrapped up, Plotkin used it as a chance to get another take of 'Heart of Mine.'

That recording was the version used on *Shot of Love*, and became its first single. Released ahead of the album in Europe, 'Heart of Mine' became a Top-10 hit in Norway. It made far less of an impression in the United States, where it came out shortly after the album, and, in hindsight, is more noteworthy for its B-side: 'The Groom's Still Waiting at the Altar.' That song's combination of insistent music and evocative lyrics hinted at a return to Dylan's mid-1960s style that many fans would've welcomed. Ironically, the song wasn't included on the album's original release, and was added only after the song started receiving significant airplay on rock radio stations.

Just as Plotkin clashed with Dylan over the album's overall sound – Dylan preferring the rough mixes to any studio polishing – they also disagreed on song selection. Though 'The Groom's Still Waiting at the Altar' was generally acknowledged as one of his best songs from the period, Dylan told Cameron Crowe that it 'sounded okay, but it wasn't really the way I wanted to play it'. Whatever Plotkin's feelings about the virtues of specific songs, his pragmatism carried through to selecting the song sequence as well. 'An album is a program of music,' he explained. 'It's not just simply the best ten songs that you wrote during that period of time. It has to add up to something.'

That said, the math for *Shot of Love* is much more favorable with 'The Groom's Still Waiting at the Altar' factored in. Despite Dylan's feeling that he and the band had 'lost the original riff to the point where it was nonexistent', the song's chugging riff gives it a visceral appeal. It also benefits from invoking religious imagery against a seemingly secular backdrop in a similar vein to a song like *Blood on the Tracks*' 'Shelter From the Storm'. Ironically – considering its initial relegation to a B-side – 'The Groom's Still Waiting at the Altar' is one of the most frequently collected from Dylan's 1980s work – appearing on at least four commercially-released compilations, plus a late-1990s promotional disc called *Words and Music*.

Coincidentally, like *Saved* the previous year, *Shot of Love* was released in a gap between tours, and critical and commercial reaction to the album turned out to be worse than that of its predecessor. *Shot of Love* missed the Top 30 in the US, and while it reached the UK Top 10, reviewer Nick Kent from *New Musical Express* called it 'Dylan's worst album to date'. Even the usually-friendly *Rolling Stone* – which had given *Saved* a largely positive review – slammed the new album, with reviewer Paul Nelson dismissing it as 'filled mainly with hatred, confusion and egoism.'

When Dylan returned to touring in June 1981, he didn't work especially hard to build up anticipation for the new record ahead of its debut. Nearly all of the album's songs were performed live at some point on the 1981 tour, but the initial shows only included three of them. The title track wasn't played live until a dozen shows into the tour (somewhat surprisingly, considering how pleased he was with its studio incarnation) – during a concert at Earl's Court in London on 1 July – and ultimately appeared in less than half of the year's setlists. As an album introduction, the song 'Shot of Love' set a very different tone than the cover version of 'A Satisfied Mind' had on *Saved*. Both recordings have a spontaneous feel but otherwise display few similarities. It's hard to imagine any song on *Saved* or *Slow Train Coming* including a lyric like 'Don't need a shot of heroin to kill my disease', let alone Dylan starting the album with it. The musical and lyrical directness was clearly deliberate on his part. In a 1983 interview with *New Musical Express*, he described the song as defining 'where (he was) at spiritually, musically, romantically and whatever else'.

Following a composition the singer positioned as 'not hiding anything', 'Heart of Mine' feels decidedly evasive and almost playful. While not the only song on *Shot of Love* inspired by his personal life, the jaunty rhythm and absence of the regular band ensemble make it a musical outlier. In the mid-1980s, using different musician lineups from one track to another was typical of Dylan albums; but in this period, cohesion was the norm, and typically led to better performances. He later conceded that he used this particular version for the album mainly because Ron Wood and Ringo Starr played on it.

While Dylan frequently got defensive about criticism of his religious views – on stage and in interviews – it rarely came through explicitly in his music. He made an exception in 'Property of Jesus', which, oddly enough, is a song he never performed live. Sometimes compared to his 1965 hit 'Positively 4th Street', the main difference is that whereas the older song allows for an aesthetic distance between narrator and subject, the feelings displayed in 'Property of Jesus' are raw nerves. Even with its subject being discussed in the third person, it's unlikely that anyone hearing the song envisioned that person being anyone other than Dylan.

The following track, 'Lenny Bruce', also offers a bit of biography but does so more openly and, admittedly, with less relevance to the subject matter. In the song, Dylan describes an actual event – sharing a cab with the comedian – but the song's animating spirit is bemusement at such a controversial figure being lionized in death after having been castigated in life.

They said that he was sick 'cause he didn't play by the rules
He just showed the wise men of his day to be nothing more than fools

It must've seemed like unusual subject matter at the time, and superficially it was. However, Dylan had also written his share of outlaw songs – a description that, from a certain perspective, also fits songs about Jesus. Considering the run-ins Jesus had with 'wise men' in the biblical accounts, the connection is clearer. Dylan's own sense of connection to the song also seems clear. It's the most recently performed song from *Shot of Love* by a substantial margin, having featured in the autumn 2019 leg of the Never Ending Tour.

Side One closes with another response to detractors: 'Watered-Down Love'. While certainly defiant, the tone is less combative, even when it integrates scriptural references. In the opening line, Dylan sings, 'Love that's pure hopes all things', recalling *First Corinthians'* oft-quoted declaration that 'Love bears all things, believes all things, hopes all things, endures all things'. However, this biblical conviction is portrayed as being at odds with the shallow expectations of the world at large. The contrast between earthly compromise and purity of heart is outlined in a fashion familiar to most TV viewers – with assurances that love in its worthwhile form 'won't write it up and make you sign a false confession.'

As the original Side Two opener, the main accomplishment of 'Dead Man, Dead Man' is to show how much stronger 'The Groom's Still Waiting at the Altar' makes the album as a whole. It's easy to imagine the former song being directed at the same people as 'Property of Jesus', albeit with a touch more sympathy and a more inviting, reggae-influenced rhythm. Setting your dividing line between Christian charity and castigation based on whether you're the one being attacked, was arguably at odds with Jesus in the Sermon on the Mount admonishing his followers that 'Whosoever shall smite thee on thy right cheek, turn to him the other also'. But by this point, anyone expecting complete consistency from Bob Dylan was clearly listening to the wrong artist.

The blend of secular and spiritual concerns in 'In The Summertime' is much more satisfying. Like the best of Dylan's love songs of the period, the ambiguity of the lyrical subject matter was part of the appeal. The opening lines quickly establish the wistful mood, somewhere between a dream and a memory:

> I was in your presence for an hour or so
> Or was it a day? I truly don't know

A line about a time 'before the flood', evokes not just the *Bible*, but Dylan's own past in the line's reference to the title of the live album from his 1974 tour with The Band. But for all the talk of the past, the singer has his mind on a very long-term future.

> And I'm still carrying the gift you gave
> It's a part of me now, it's been cherished and saved
> It'll be with me unto the grave
> And then unto eternity

With strong singing and harmonica-playing on Dylan's part, 'In the Summertime' is also a melodic standout – something which cannot be said of the album's penultimate song 'Trouble'. As a report on the state of the nation, it's musically and lyrically undistinguished. With only the mildest of veiled religious references, it's one of his rare songs from this period that might've felt the benefit from a bit more fire and brimstone. Live recordings show that the song works well enough in concert, but that view came late and departed quickly – all of its total of seven performances took place across a four-month period in 1989.

From the ordinary to the sublime, *Shot of Love* closes with the one universally acclaimed song from this period. The perception that Dylan's religious songs were completely literal expressions of his own views rarely worked in his favor, but 'Every Grain of Sand' is an exception to the rule. Singing 'Every hair is numbered like Every Grain of Sand', evokes the 'Gospel of Matthew', which also inspired William Blake's 'Auguries of Innocence' as consciously as 'Dead Man, Dead Man' seemed to ignore its lessons in tolerance. Likewise, the humility expressed in the opening lines – 'In the time of my confession / In the hour of my deepest need' – sets the stage for some revelatory wordplay later.

> I hear the ancient footsteps like the motion of the sea
> Sometimes I turn, there's someone there, other times it's only me

Even many reviewers who disliked the album as a whole, praised this particular song. This included *Rolling Stone*'s Paul Nelson, whose generally negative review nonetheless described how the song made 'the gates of Heaven dissolve into a universality that has nothing to do with most of the LP'. The acclaim for Dylan's performance of it also serves as a reminder of the unusual turns that typify his career.

As with the songs that became *Slow Train Coming*, Dylan intended for 'Every Grain of Sand' to be recorded by another singer – in this case Nana Mouskouri. She eventually recorded it for her 1986 album *Why Worry* – a collection of pop songs that opened with Mark Knopfler's Dylanesque title track and closed with 'Every Grain of Sand'. Dylan's own attempts to record the song went back to the previous September and a demo recorded at Rundown Studios with backing vocals by Jennifer Warnes. Everyone who heard the song or read the lyrics seemed to recognize it as something special, and unlike 'Caribbean Wind' or other ambitious but abandoned songs, Dylan actually recognized this quality himself and stayed the course.

Describing the process of writing this 'inspired song' in the liner notes for *Biograph*, he recalled feeling 'like I was just putting words down that were coming from somewhere else, and I just stuck it out'. He elaborated on this with Bill Flanagan:

> In a song like that, there's no consciousness of any of this stuff having been said before. 'What's this like?' Well, it's not like anything. 'What does it represent?' Well, you don't even know. All you know is that it's a

mood piece, and you try to hold onto the mood and finish. Or not even finish, but just get it to a place where you can let it go. Because those kinds of things, you'll never finish if you don't do them all at one period of time.

The hero of the performance released on *Shot of Love* is Chuck Plotkin, who showed his commitment as a producer when Dylan spontaneously started playing the song at the piano. Realizing that there was no microphone set up to capture the vocal, and that he couldn't count on the singer being willing to record another take, Plotkin grabbed a microphone and held it while Dylan sang. For whatever reason, the song wasn't played live until 21 November 1981: the final show of the fall 1981 tour.

Shortly after completing this enduring profession of his faith, Bob Dylan became embroiled in a secular matter tied to a relationship far older than those with any of his female associates. On 18 May, former manager Albert Grossman filed a lawsuit over unpaid royalties and commissions. Apparently viewing the preservation of earthly treasure as fully compatible with attaining the kingdom of heaven, Dylan undertook an aggressive legal response intended to outlast Grossman financially. The matter would not be settled until six years later.

London was the site for six of Dylan's 1981 concerts, the most of any venue on the tour. Though he remained popular in England – arguably more so than in the United States – his shows received unfavorable comparisons to those of Bruce Springsteen, who had played six shows at Wembley Arena a few weeks earlier. The nature of rock music's narrative made this understandable if not necessarily deserved, at least based on the recordings that have been released. Dylan's setlists retained the balance between newer compositions and pre-conversion material, and while there had been some turnover in the band, Jim Keltner, Tim Drummond and Fred Tackett remained at its core.

From the UK, the tour continued to continental Europe. Unfortunately, the European shows ended on a tragic note when, on 25 July, two fans died at an outdoor show in the French town of Avignon.

When the band returned to the road in October, *Shot of Love* was dropping down the *Billboard* chart, and Al Kooper had taken over as keyboard player. Dylan's revived connection with his past took another step when filmmaker Howard Alk started traveling with the tour. Alk – whose friendship with Dylan began in the early-1960s – collaborated with him on editing the 1972 film *Eat the Document,* and also 1978's infamous

Renaldo and Clara which he also helped shoot. While *Renaldo and Clara* – with its semi-narrative account of the Rolling Thunder Revue – had been poorly received, Dylan indulged Alk's efforts to film new material in a similar vein during the 1981 tour. Just as nothing more came of this material, nothing more came of the band after the tour concluded in November 1981. While Dylan would work with some of these musicians again in the future, this particular ensemble had run its course. 'When the holidays came, it was just a tough time,' commented Arthur Rosato. 'I came right back down again and talked to Bob. Bob realized it was the end of an era. We just all packed up and said goodbye.'

One of the most striking things about this part of Bob Dylan's career, is that it's one of his last truly prolific songwriting periods: a circumstance that shaped some of his records later in the decade. From the conclusion of the initial gospel tour in May 1980, through the main recording sessions for *Shot of Love*, Dylan experts have cataloged more than 30 new songs that could've appeared on the album. Of these, only about a dozen were serious contenders for the album; though he also recorded some covers at Clover, including 'Let It Be Me' and the R&B classic 'Mystery Train'. Dylan had recorded the former song – a 1959 Top-10 hit for the Everly Brothers – a decade earlier for the album *Self Portrait*. The new rendition – effectively a duet with Clydie King – was the B-side of the European 'Heart of Mine' single, making 'Let It Be Me' one of the few *Shot of Love* outtakes released contemporaneously. Others would have to wait anywhere from four years to nearly four decades for official releases.

Following *Biograph*'s inclusion of 'Caribbean Wind' and an excellent live performance of 'Heart of Mine', the initial 1991 set from the ongoing *Bootleg Series* offered three *Shot of Love* outtakes plus the initial 'Every Grain of Sand' demo. While the album version of that song is superior – if only slightly more polished – the early rendition shows the song to be every bit as inspired as Dylan claimed. The arrangement may have needed refinement, but minor changes aside, it was fully formed lyrically.

The three outtakes differ greatly in style and substance. 'You Changed My Life' is the most straightforward in its expression of devotion. Its subject matter is apparent well before the final verse line 'My Lord and my Savior', with lyrics drawing a sharp contrast between 'silver and gold and what man cannot hold.'

You do the work of the devil
You got a million friends

They'll be there when you got something
They'll take it all in the end

At the same time, there's a joy to the music, and comparing the source of
his salvation to Errol Flynn implies a desire to reach beyond the already
faithful. The biggest surprise about the song isn't so much that Dylan left
it off *Shot of Love*, as that he never played it in concert.

The bluesy 'Need a Woman' veers back toward earthly matters, though
his spiritual concerns remain deeply intertwined. 'Searching for the truth
the way God designed it' was at least on par with other considerations.
The song got a second life thanks to Tim Drummond and Jim Keltner –
the duo suggested the song to Ry Cooder while working with him on his
1982 album *The Slide Area*. The guitarist liked the song well enough to
record it, albeit with a variety of lyric changes. 'I had to focus because
he's so vague,' he recalled in the album's liner notes. 'His words go in
all directions. 'I can't do this,' I thought – 'I must make a story out of it'.'
Cooder added that Dylan had no objections to the lyric changes.

With its keyboard-focused arrangement and lyrics recalling a past
that showcases the distinction between facts and truth, 'Angelina' calls
to mind both 'Lenny Bruce' and 'In The Summertime.' Of the *Shot of
Love* outtakes featured on the initial *Bootleg Series* release, 'Angelina'
came closest to appearing on the final album. Chuck Plotkin pushed
for its inclusion, but Dylan overruled him: a decision widely viewed as
diminishing the album. One can certainly make a case for 'Angelina' over
some of the songs on *Shot of Love*; however, it's a more equivocal case
than its partisans maintain. Some powerful lines (such as 'When you cease
to exist, then who will you blame') are offset by the pains to which Dylan
goes to find rhymes for the title – from 'concertina' to 'Argentina,' the
words dictate the narrative, making the composition feel a bit schematic.

Most subsequent releases from the *Bootleg Series* focus on
acknowledged high points like the Rolling Thunder Revue or the
Basement Tapes. The thirteenth volume – 2017's *Trouble No More* –
unapologetically spotlights the born-again period. The core of *Trouble
No More* is live performances from 1979 to 1981, with the deluxe edition
featuring several songs written between *Saved* and *Shot of Love*. These
compositions – presented in a mix of concert and rehearsal recordings –
are largely undistinguished. Though presumably written with the stage
in mind, only the slow burn of 'Making a Liar' and the dynamic 'Yonder
Comes Sin' catch fire. 'City of Gold' is clearly striving for some sort of

DECADES | Bob Dylan in the 80s

transcendence, but neither the melody nor the lyric achieve it. Of the others, 'Jesus Is the One,' 'Thief on the Cross' and 'Rise Again' sound more like outtakes from *Slow Train Coming* or *Saved* that deserved to remain outtakes.

Road-testing overtly evangelical songs at a point where more-nuanced compositions like 'Every Grain of Sand' remained in the studio, paints an ambivalent portrait of his faith. Bob Dylan's related ambivalence about the path his music should take, was matched by an empirical lack of interest in that question among his audience. Coincidentally or not, the following year would be the among the least active of his entire career.

1982: Other Times It's Only Me

If the 1980s were Bob Dylan's lost decade, 1982 stands out as his lost year within this era, at least from a public standpoint. The singer made just one single concert appearance during the entire year – the first year since 1972 where he released no new music. At the end of 1981 – following three years packed with regular writing, recording and touring – Dylan had already confided to people close to him that he was considering a longer break before starting on another album or tour. A tragic start to the new year solidified that intention.

After the *Shot of Love* tour ended, Howard Alk continued discussing potential film projects with Dylan, though the singer's actual level of commitment was ambiguous. For Alk, this took place against a backdrop of drug problems and the dissolution of his second marriage. While the latter led to him setting up makeshift living quarters at Rundown Studios around Christmas 1981, the former led to him overdosing on heroin there sometime between Christmas and New Year's Day. His body was discovered at the studio early in January. Despite the coroner ruling the death an accident, some of those close to Alk believed it to be suicide – an interpretation bolstering his own comments from shortly before his death. This cohort included Alk's first wife, Jones, who had worked on D. A. Pennebaker's documentary *Don't Look Back* along with her ex-husband. She expressed her doubts about Alk's death in an interview with biographer Howard Sounes: 'It is possible that, by mistake, he killed himself. Sometimes junkies do. But I think that (he) killed himself (deliberately).'

Howard Alk's death expedited Dylan's decision to shut down Rundown. However, he was already leaning toward the same decision before these tragic events. With no imminent plans to tour or work on new songs, the singer had little need for rehearsal space or his own studio. He eventually moved the Rundown recording equipment into his Malibu home. That decision set the stage for one of his career's great happy accidents several years later, when his friend George Harrison asked him about using the space to work on a new song.

Prior to moving the equipment, there were still a few sessions held at Rundown itself. In addition to a February 1982 jam session with Allen Ginsberg, playing on the poet's song 'Do the Meditation Rock', Dylan spent a June afternoon trying out musical ideas with drummer Bruce Gary. Like his friend Jim Keltner, Gary performed with a wide variety of artists in his career. He also recorded three albums as a member of The Knack, helping devise the distinctive rhythm of their international hit 'My Sharona'. At Keltner's invitation, Gary played with the band for two shows of the *Shot of Love* tour in New Orleans, and gained Dylan's appreciation for '(breathing) some new life into the shows.'

The five-year lease on the Rundown building more or less coincided with the five-year/five-album record deal Dylan had signed in 1978. Though he didn't renew the lease, he did sign another five-year/five-album recording contract with Columbia, albeit with an inauspicious start. The label apparently rejected his first new project – a collection of duets recorded with Clydie King – because it didn't 'fall into any category that the record company knows how to deal with.' Clydie King may have been Bob Dylan's primary romantic interest at the time, but she wasn't the only one. At his son Samuel's bar mitzvah, he met Carole Childs, who was attending as the guest of David Geffen. Dylan's relationship with Childs, then working in Geffen Records' A&R department, endured to some degree until 1992.

For most fathers, attending their son's bar mitzvah would hardly be noteworthy regardless of their own faith. However, even amid diminished popularity and critical stature, Bob Dylan exerted an unusual fascination, and the event was seized upon as evidence of another shift in religious belief. A piece in the 15 March edition of *New York Magazine* titled 'Dylan Ditching Gospel?' encouraged speculation that the singer declining an invitation to present the National Music Publishers Association's award for Gospel Song of the Year signified a move away from Christianity. This was not the first time people questioned the sincerity of Dylan's faith, which remains a matter of debate to the present day. Even some of those close to the singer expressed skepticism about his motives. Along with Keith Richards' oft-quoted description of Dylan being the 'prophet of profit' in this period, a sharper (if not necessarily more thoughtful) assessment came from Ronnie Hawkins. Describing a 1980 encounter on the gospel tour, Hawkins recalled, 'I knew what he was doing. And he knew I knew what he was doing – he was selling records.'

Perhaps Hawkins would've taken a different view had this conversation taken place after *Saved* became the worst-selling Bob Dylan album in fifteen years. If his religious stance had truly been as cynical as Hawkins' opinion of it supposed, adopting it would rank as one of the biggest failures of the singer's career. The idea that even an artist as mercurial as Dylan would purposely subject himself to derision on so many fronts for so long simply as a publicity stunt, strains credulity. Looking back on this period, Arthur Rosato recently commented, '(Dylan) stood by every word and every note during that time, but it wore on him.'

In the book *The Gospel According to Bob Dylan*, writer Michael J. Gilmour contrasted the reaction to Dylan's conversion against the milder public responses to declarations of faith by peers such as George Harrison and Cat Stevens (now known as Yusuf Islam). Gilmour attributes the differing responses to broader perceptions of the religions in question: Hinduism and Islam respectively. Both faiths were viewed at the time as somewhat exotic and thus more in keeping with an artistic path. Conversely, the type of fundamentalist Christianity that Dylan embraced, invited associations with narrow-mindedness and intolerance, and the singer's public comments often played into that impression.

The reaction to Yusuf Islam's 1989 comments about the death threats against author Salman Rushdie related to the novel *The Satanic Verses* are the exception that proves the rule. When Yusuf seemingly endorsed calls for Rushdie's death because of alleged blasphemous depictions of the Islamic faith – and the prophet Mohammed in particular – many fans saw it as an affront to freedom of speech. Though Yusuf had retired from performing after his conversion to Islam, the backlash was significant, with numerous radio stations refusing to play his records, and the band 10,000 Maniacs removing a cover version of his song 'Peace Train' from their recent album *In My Tribe*. Even in his fiercest onstage declarations during the gospel tours, Dylan never generated quite the same level of uproar, but one imagines he could empathize with the former Cat Stevens.

One of the key points Gilmour discusses in relation to Dylan, is the idea that faith tends to be a process of discovery. The term 'born-again' sometimes carries connotations of flipping a switch rather than starting a process of discovery. Dylan's comments to Karen Hughes in 1980 about having 'to learn all over again' acknowledged this aspect. But, ironically, many of those questioning the substance of his faith, seem not to have considered it.

Examining the interplay between artistry and faith in his book *Dylan – What Happened?*, Paul Williams posited that there are actually two Bob Dylans. Williams envisioned the 'inner man' and the 'outer man' – both of them very spiritual but engaging with it in very different ways. Where the inner man struggled to embrace a newfound relationship with a higher power, the outer man – described by Williams as 'nothing but the outer shell of Bob Dylan' – simply mimicked the expected attitudes of a born-again Christian.

Bearing in mind the divergence between plaintive songs like 'What Can I Do For You?' and the aggressive end-times rhetoric presented on stage, Williams' premise provides a compelling framework for understanding the evolution of Dylan's music in this era. Ironically, as the inner man's expressions of faith were, on balance, becoming more sophisticated – wrestling with ambiguity but still exuding tangible passion – the number of people actually hearing them, continued to shrink.

Amid the uncertainty about his musical future, Dylan nevertheless accepted recognition for his previous work. On 24 January, at a ceremony in New York City, he was inducted into the Songwriters Hall of Fame. This was one of just two public events he participated in that year.

The other was a brief live performance with Joan Baez at Peace Sunday: a concert promoting nuclear disarmament. The show took place on 6 June at the Rose Bowl in Pasadena, California, in front of an estimated audience of 85,000. While most of that crowd was probably there for Jackson Browne, Stevie Nicks and Stevie Wonder – all of whom were selling far more records at the time – they responded enthusiastically when Baez introduced Dylan. Together, the pair sang 'With God on Our Side,' 'Blowin' in the Wind' and Jimmy Buffett's 'A Pirate Looks at Forty'. Dylan playing a song by another current artist rather than something of his own – religious or otherwise – might've surprised some of those watching, but he had been keeping up to date with popular music. On his 1980 and 1981 tours, he performed Dave Mason's 1977 hit 'We Just Disagree' periodically, and one way he spent the summer of 1982 was by going to punk and new wave shows in Minnesota with his oldest son Jesse. In addition to The Clash, Squeeze and X, the artists they saw included Elvis Costello and The Attractions. When Dylan was ready to start working on a new album, Costello was reputedly one of the people he asked about producing it with him.

Though it's unclear how seriously Dylan discussed the prospect of working on the album with Costello or in fact David Bowie, he talked to at least one potential producer at length. In an interview with journalist Karl Dallas, Frank Zappa described Bob Dylan showing up at his house unannounced shortly before Christmas 1982. During the visit, Dylan played some new songs for Zappa on the piano and asked if he'd be interested in working together. Zappa was apparently interested, in principle, but nothing further came of it except speculation about what such an album would've been like, and rumors of tapes from the meeting (supposedly recorded by Zappa's engineer Mark Pinske).

The rationale for approaching Costello and other artists appears to be much the same as for *Shot of Love* – a desire to find someone conversant with studio technology who also appreciated the value of live performance. Perhaps Dylan felt that someone who was primarily a performer would be more receptive to his priorities than Chuck Plotkin or the tandem of Jerry Wexler and Barry Beckett had been. Dylan's ultimate choice as co-producer of the album that became *Infidels* wasn't as famous as the others he asked, but was nonetheless an artist in their own right who probably gave the singer the comfort that his latest songs would be in safe hands.

1983: The World Could Come To an End Tonight

In the context of a 1983 interview with Martin Keller for the *Minneapolis City Pages*, Dylan gave this discourse on his religious background:

> My so-called Jewish roots are in Egypt – they went down there with Joseph, and they came back out with Moses, you know, the guy that killed the Egyptian, married an Ethiopian girl, and brought the law down from the mountain. The same Moses whose staff turned into a serpent – the same person who killed 3,000 Hebrews for getting down, stripping off their clothes and dancing around a golden calf. These are my roots.

Dylan punctuated this by offering the declaration, 'I ain't looking for them in synagogues'. In the process, he aptly demonstrated that when it comes to speculation about matters of personal faith, his own comments rarely bring the question into sharper focus.

The same is true of his actions. In 1983, these included a trip to Jerusalem for his seventeen-year-old son Jesse's belated bar mitzvah, and spending time learning about Judaism with the Hasidic sect Chabad Lubavitch. As with Samuel's bar mitzvah the previous year, taking part in such a solemn occasion should hardly have attracted any attention, never mind debate, but the setting's religious significance made it virtually inevitable.

The intrigue around Dylan's association with Chabad-Lubavitch – a group whose history went back to 18th-century Poland – was more understandable. While many Hasidic sects self-segregate, the Lubavitchers were known for outreach to the broader Jewish community – especially non-observant Jews. When one of the group's rabbis Kasriel Kastel was asked about Dylan's faith for a 1984 article in *Christianity Today*, he replied, 'As far as we're concerned, he was a confused Jew. We feel he's coming back.' Dylan himself offered no direct comment on the subject, but maintained a relationship with the group for many years, and appeared at several of their annual To Life telethons.

Dylan's most enduring activity in 1983 was the recording and release of the album *Infidels*. Though not a runaway hit, it was his best-received record in several years, and by some measures, his most successful of the decade. However, like most things involving Bob Dylan, this is far from a straightforward proposition. Other than *Blood on the Tracks* – where the singer re-recorded half the album at the test-pressing stage – none of his records have received as much scrutiny from Dylanologists about which songs should've been included. Fittingly, when *Infidels* was released, many reviewers used *Blood on the Tracks* as a proxy to signify Dylan's previous artistic high points. The reviews themselves ranged from glowing to dismissive, with Graham Lock of *New Musical Express,* and *Rolling Stone*'s Christopher Connelly, reflecting the extremes. Lock characterized *Infidels* as the work of 'a confused man trying to rekindle old fires', while Connelly called the album 'a stunning recovery of the lyric and melodic powers that seemed to have all but deserted him'. Stephen Holden from the *New York Times* offered a more measured assessment, taking issue with what he perceived as a misanthropic tone, yet praising the album's better songs for blending the vivid imagery of Dylan's 1960s work with the religious fervor of his more recent compositions.

Another common thread in reviews was praise for the album's overall sound and the assembled musicians who made it a reality – especially Dire Straits guitarist and producer Mark Knopfler, who had previously played on *Slow Train Coming*. Accounts vary as to whether producer Jerry Wexler or Dylan himself had suggested Knopfler for the 1979 album. Wexler and Barry Beckett produced Dire Straits' second album *Communique* in late-1978, while Dylan supposedly approached the guitarist after seeing the band perform in Los Angeles in March 1979, so either story sounds plausible. Regardless of the actual backstory, the pair worked well together – even if Knopfler was initially taken aback by the new songs' religious content – and his guitar work was often cited as a positive in reviews of *Slow Train Coming*.

Despite having a massive hit with 'Sultans of Swing,' Dire Straits' popularity in the United States lagged behind the UK and other European countries. This would change in the summer of 1985 when the album *Brothers in Arms* and its MTV-driven single 'Money for Nothing' made Dire Straits one of the world's biggest bands. In the spring of 1983 though, they were simply a solidly successful group, whose leader had begun a well-received sideline in composing film scores. Knopfler's soundtrack album for the cult-favorite *Local Hero* was released the month before recording sessions for *Infidels* started.

If approaching Frank Zappa and other more-acclaimed musicians implied that Knopfler wasn't Dylan's top choice to make the album with, the singer was nevertheless exceedingly complimentary publicly about the guitarist's contribution. 'Mark was incredible,' Dylan told Martin Keller. 'He helped make this record in a thousand ways, not only musically, which in itself would have been enough. Brilliant guy, I can't say enough about him.'

Knopfler was central to the sound of *Infidels* on multiple fronts, but its musical richness reflects the collective input of one of Dylan's more eclectic studio bands – one where most of the musicians were artists in their own right. The Jamaican duo of drummer Sly Dunbar and bassist Robbie Shakespeare provided a solid rhythmic foundation, and remain two of reggae's most respected musicians and acclaimed producers. Dylan also recruited former Rolling Stones guitarist Mick Taylor, who he'd met via Bruce Gary the year before. Knopfler bringing in Dire Straits' keyboardist Alan Clark and engineer Neil Dorfsman ensured the record would have some of the same sonic polish as a Dire Straits album – but the overall result still sounded unique.

Infidels (1983)

Personnel:
Bob Dylan: vocals, guitar, harmonica and keyboards
Sly Dunbar: drums and percussion
Robbie Shakespeare: bass
Mick Taylor: guitar
Mark Knopfler: guitar
Alan Clark: Keyboards
Clydie King: vocals ('Union Sundown')
Producers: Bob Dylan, Mark Knopfler
Engineer: Josh Abbey
Release date: US: 27 October 1983, UK: 4 November 1983
Chart places: US: 20, UK: 9
Running time: 41:39
All songs written by Bob Dylan.

Side One: 1. 'Jokerman' 2. 'Sweetheart Like You' 3. 'Neighborhood Bully' 4. 'License To Kill'
Side Two: 1. 'Man of Peace' 2. 'Union Sundown' 3. 'I And I' 4. 'Don't Fall Apart On Me Tonight'

As with any Dylan album, *Infidels*' identity is rooted in the songs. In April, the band started recording at New York City studio the Power Station, with an impressive collection of new compositions, many of which Dylan had started writing while sailing the Caribbean on the Water Pearl. At the same time, the record reflects a shift in his songwriting approach – one only made possible by the studio technology he treated with ambivalence for so long. Dylan once remarked that he didn't learn about overdubbing until 1978 – a possibly facetious acknowledgment that once he recorded a song – generally with a live-in-the-studio approach – its elements were locked in place, at least until he played it in concert. Having previously abandoned some captivating songs – such as 'Caribbean Wind' – because of trouble finishing the lyrics, he now used the ability to re-record vocal parts to rewrite songs, sometimes well after the main recording sessions had finished. This was in addition to rewrites the singer made throughout the sessions, which were characterized by a mix of persistence and spontaneity. Alan Clark described Dylan writing several new lines of lyrics for a new song and going right into playing it; while Sly Dunbar told Howard Sounes that he didn't realize they were recording 'Jokerman' when Dylan told the band they'd delivered the take he wanted.

Quickly recording workable versions of 'Jokerman' and 'License To Kill' – the latter recorded in a single take – stood in stark contrast to the genesis of other tracks, which were more labored. In a 1984 interview for *Guitar Player* magazine, Mark Knopfler talked about working on *Infidels*:

> One of the great parts about production, is that it demonstrates that you have to be flexible ... Each song has its own secret that's different from another song, and each has its own life. Sometimes it has to be teased out, whereas other times, it might come fast.

Even with that mindset, the guitarist probably hadn't anticipated devoting full days in the studio to individual songs, or recording over a dozen takes of songs that were ultimately left off the album.

But the bigger surprise for Knopfler came in October 1983 when *Infidels* was released in a very different form to what he and Dylan crafted earlier in the year. After recording about 20 songs, the pair settled on a sequence of nine songs for the album in early May, prior to Knopfler and Clark leaving on a European tour with Dire Straits. Knopfler offered to complete the final mix after the tour. But the following month, Dylan returned to the Power Station without Knopfler and reworked individual tracks and the overall album sequence – removing two songs and substituting a single new one in their place.

In a 1984 interview with MTV VJ Martha Quinn, Dylan attributed this decision to a worry that the album as recorded felt predictable, implicitly contradicting the earlier praise for his former collaborator. Asked about its recording for a 2016 article in the magazine *Uncut*, engineer Neil Dorfsman identified the sessions devoted to instrumental overdubs as the point when he believed Dylan began 'rethinking' the album. Knopfler's comments about the experience betray understandable disappointment on his part, but the guitarist generally took the high road while maintaining that the record would've been better had he gotten the chance to complete his work. By 1986, whatever strain the events put on their relationship had sufficiently eased enough for Dylan to make a guest appearance at a Dire Straits concert, and in 2011, the pair shared billing on a European tour, as well as playing selected songs together on a North American tour in 2012.

Among the songs Dylan rewrote lyrics and re-recorded vocals for, was the opening track (and the first song composed for the album) 'Jokerman'. Presuming that the singer's claim that he hated the way the song sounded when he heard it playing in a record store, was sincere, it represents one of the more profound disconnects between an artist's perception of their work and the view of their audience. 'Jokerman' has been performed infrequently in concert – and not since 2003 – but has appeared on nearly as many compilations as 'The Groom's Still Waiting at the Altar'. Dylan described it in a 1991 interview as, 'a song that got away from me', yet polls by critics and fans consistently rank it as one of his best songs from the decade.

Though more lyrically impressionistic, 'Jokerman' works in much in the same vein as 'Caribbean Wind', with the 'distant ships sailing into the mist' possibly part of the same fleet as the earlier song's 'distant ships of liberty'. Intended or not, beginning the album with this particular song, provided a *de facto* response to the ongoing speculation surrounding the singer's faith. The biblical overtones and concern with the end times remain, but *Infidels* established that Dylan now embraced those elements on his own terms, rather than those of the Vineyard Fellowship or any other denomination.

Well, the book of Leviticus and Deuteronomy
The law of the jungle and the sea are your only teachers
In the smoke of the twilight on a milk-white steed
Michelangelo indeed could have carved out your features
Resting in the fields, far from the turbulent space
Half asleep near the stars with a small dog licking your face

The second track, 'Sweetheart Like You' shows how well-matched Dylan and Knopfler were musically at this point. A more secular companion to 'Covenant Woman' from *Saved*, echoes of this ballad can be heard in some of Mark Knopfler's more Dylanesque moments on the next Dire Straits album, such as 'Why Worry?'. While 'Sweetheart Like You' only reached number 55 when released as a single in the US, it's better-known for two sections in the lyric – one highly praised, and the other frequently deployed to question Dylan's attitudes about women. The latter comes midway through the song:

> You know, a woman like you should be at home
> That's where you belong
> Taking care of somebody nice
> Who don't know how to do you wrong

After a decade of raw emotional expression and outright evangelizing, the singer had lost the benefit of the doubt about whether the narrative voice of his songs reflected his own feelings. Asked about these specific lines in a 1984 *Rolling Stone* interview with Kurt Loder, Dylan admitted that they didn't come across the way he wanted, but added that any changes he could have made, wouldn't have changed the song's overall tone. The slightly different wording published on his official website, bears this out:

> You know, a woman like you should be at home
> That's where you belong
> Taking care of somebody true
> Who would never do you wrong

To what extent this verse (which was dropped for the song's later usage in the stage musical *Girl From the North Country*) reflects any outright sexism on Dylan's part, is a more open question. The singer's comments in this area over the years have varied wildly. Having decried female performers who 'whore themselves' on stage in a 1987 interview, several years later, he complimented Madonna's talent and the work that went into her success. In the same interview where he equivocated about the lyrics of 'Sweetheart Like You', those comments were proceeded by the observation, 'I think women rule the world, and that no man has ever done anything that a woman either hasn't allowed him to do or encouraged him to do.'

One stanza, the acclaim of which needs no equivocation, begins the song's final verse:

> They say that patriotism is the last refuge
> To which a scoundrel clings
> Steal a little and they throw you in jail
> Steal a lot and they make you king

The next two songs demonstrate that the alternation between the genuine insight and scattershot viewpoints of 'Sweetheart Like You', was a recurring feature of *Infidels*. Despite being the album's weakest tracks, they effectively demonstrate the folly of judging Bob Dylan's work solely on his lyrics and one's own preconceptions. On the page, 'Neighborhood Bully' – which is commonly interpreted as a rambling defense of Israel's position relative to its Arab neighbors – simply comes across as strident. On record – the only place Dylan's take on the song exists, since he's never performed it on stage – his delivery gives it more dimension, allowing a degree of sarcasm to come through. Likewise, the band's performance displays a level of conviction beyond what the lyric sheet puts forth.

On vinyl, 'License To Kill' ended the first side of *Infidels*. More reflective if not necessarily more cogent than 'Neighborhood Bully', 'License To Kill' was another song that virtually invited listeners to poke at the lyrics and question their meaning. While this perhaps undersold how effectively the album intertwined the words and music, finding Dylan's lyrics to be worth analyzing rather than dismissing them for reasons of dogma, was a sign that fans found the songs to be more substantial, or at least expected them to be.

The discussion primarily targeted the couplet, 'Oh, man has invented his doom / First step was touching the moon.' Unlike his response about 'Sweetheart Like You', Dylan didn't hedge on expressing his feelings when Kurt Loder asked him about these lyrics. Instead, he offered a lengthy commentary on the notion of progress:

> I mean, what's the purpose of going to the moon? To me, it doesn't make any sense. Now they're going to put a space station up there, and it's gonna cost, what, $600 billion, $700 billion? And who's gonna benefit from it? Drug companies who are gonna be able to make better drugs. Does that make sense? Is that supposed to be something that a person

is supposed to get excited about? Is that progress? I don't think they're going to get better drugs. I think they're going to get more expensive drugs.

Dylan continued by expressing concern about the prevalence of computers and what he saw as a push to make the world 'a big global country'. Those concerns informed much of *Infidels*, but for the most part, his sentiments come across more effectively – and display a stronger affinity with his older work – when speaking to human nature in general. While the lines 'All he believes are his eyes / And his eyes they just tell him lies' don't deliver the same impact as more iconic songs like 'Ballad of a Thin Man', the thematic link is tangible.

Despite the broader range of subject matter, calling the album *Infidels* leaned into questions about religious matters. But, fittingly, the title had a far more down-to-earth rationale. Dylan told Kurt Loder, 'I wanted to call it *Surviving in a Ruthless World*. But someone pointed out that the last bunch of albums I'd made all started with the letter S. So, I said, 'Well, I don't wanna get bogged down in the letter S.' And then *Infidels* came into my head one day.' Anyone hoping to attach deeper meaning to the title was disappointed when the singer added, 'I don't know what it means, or anything.'

The album's second side begins with another pair of warnings about the state of the world. The first is among the *Infidels* songs most overtly inspired by the *Bible*: 'Man of Peace'. Its repeated refrain, 'Sometimes Satan comes as a Man of Peace', derives from the warning in the 'Book of Corinthians'' second chapter about 'false apostles' who come when 'Satan himself is transformed into an angel of light'. A musical and spiritual cousin of 'Gotta Serve Somebody', the lyrics for 'Man of Peace' actually verge on playfulness at times:

Well, he can be fascinating, he can be dull
He can ride down Niagara Falls in the barrels of your skull
I can smell something cooking
I can tell there's going to be a feast
You know that sometimes Satan comes as a Man of Peace

Like 'Man of Peace', 'Union Sundown' benefits from the band's breakneck performance, aided by vocalist Clydie King. However, where the former song's telling details portray a compelling and relatable end-times vision of a world gone wrong, the latter feels like an abstraction, despite an of-the-moment setting. This virtual state-of-the-union address harkens back to Dylan's 'North Country Blues'. The singer first played that composition (about a mining town's way of life being decimated when corporate bosses move their operations to South America, where they can pay workers less) during his appearance at the 1963 Newport Folk Festival. Two decades later, he saw a similar pattern at work with a wider range of culprits. While comparison to 'North Country Blues' makes 'Union Sundown' sensible within Dylan's body of work, the later song has less impact because its scenario seems ripped from the headlines, rather than being a reflection of anyone's individual experience.

> Well, the job that you used to have
> They gave it to somebody down in El Salvador
> The unions are big business, friend
> And they're goin' out like a dinosaur

Bob Dylan wasn't the only rock star expressing muddled sociopolitical views – especially in the 1980s – but rightly or wrongly, listeners expected more of him based on his past work. As a writer, he was on much more solid ground for *Infidels'* last two songs. According to an oft-told story, when Leonard Cohen asked Dylan how long it took him to write 'I and I', he claimed to have done so in fifteen minutes. Regardless of the anecdote's accuracy, Dylan connected with something in 'I and I', which remains the most frequently performed *Infidels* song. He played it throughout his brief European tour in 1984, and in shows on the 1986 and 1987 tours with Tom Petty and The Heartbreakers, then revisited the song periodically in the 1990s. 'That was one of them Caribbean songs,' he told Paul Zollo in a 1991 interview for the magazine *SongTalk*. 'One year, a bunch of songs just came to me hanging around down in the islands, and that was one of them.' The title comes from a Rastafarian expression signifying the belief that God is within everyone. Because a corollary to this view is the idea that all people are united, Rastafarians sometimes use the phrase in place of the word 'we'. Dylan plays off of this dual meaning with the lyric 'Someone else is speakin' with my mouth, but I'm listening only to my heart.'

The aura of foreboding where 'The world could come to an end tonight,' sets the stage for the other *Infidels* love song. Gentle and lilting, but never syrupy, if 'Don't Fall Apart on Me Tonight' doesn't exactly end the album on a hopeful note, it at least conveys that focusing on the world to come, doesn't preclude meaningful connections in the here-and-now. Though not as melodically delicate as 'Sweetheart Like You,' it avoids that song's patriarchal missteps (Two of the better-known covers are by female artists) and is a relatively rare case of a biographical interpretation working to the singer's credit.

When DJ Dave Herman, in a 1981 radio interview, asked Dylan about other worthwhile paths he could've taken, Dylan replied, 'Like become a doctor... who can save somebody's life on the highway. I mean, that's a man I'm gonna look up to as being somebody with some talent.' Two years later, that sentiment resurfaced as an impassioned declaration in verse two of 'Don't Fall Apart on Me Tonight':

I wish I'd have been a doctor
Maybe I'd have saved some life that had been lost
Maybe I'd have done some good in the world
'Stead of burning every bridge I crossed

Dylan's harmonica-playing leads the song from start to finish. Whether intended or not, using the harmonica to punctuate the album's ending, fits with the concept of *Infidels* as an artistic comeback. That his reference to burning bridges could refer just as well to the toll the born-again period had taken on his career as it did to his shambolic personal life, likewise suggested a return to form.

Another area where *Infidels* differed from its immediate predecessors, was in concert. After a trio of albums where collectively just a single song wasn't played live at some point, *Infidels* includes three songs Dylan has never performed on stage. What makes this surprising – beyond the quality of the compositions – is the singer's later comments about how the songs were better before he tampered with them in the studio. In light of his conviction that songs reveal themselves in performance, playing them in concert would've been an ideal forum to reconnect with some of his finest compositions.

As for the songs recorded for but left off of *Infidels*, some were reworked for his next album *Empire Burlesque*, and a cover of Willie Nelson's 'Angel Flying Too Close To The Ground' became the B-side of the 'Union Sundown' single, which briefly charted in the UK. Others remained the province of bootlegs and, of course, *The Bootleg Series*. With five outtakes, *Infidels* was among the albums most thoroughly represented on *The Bootleg Series*' inaugural 1991 release. The first of these outtakes – 'Someone's Got a Hold of My Heart' – underwent a combination of major lyric rewriting and assorted overdubs to become *Empire Burlesque*'s opening track 'Tight Connection to My Heart'. The next two – 'Tell Me' and 'Lord Protect the Child' – are solid songs, but not necessarily better than anything on the album as released. The remaining two outtakes remain the subject of passionate debate on that point.

The first time many fans heard 'Foot of Pride' was when Lou Reed performed it at the Bob Dylan tribute concert held at Madison Square Garden in October 1992. Like the best Dylan covers, Reed's rendition feels like a fusion of both the performer and the writer's sensibilities. While Reed isn't known for invoking biblical language (The title is derived from the Book of Psalms), his affinity for human foibles – not to mention the lyric reference to 'a woman who passes herself off as a male' – made this diatribe a perfect fit.

Where Reed's approach to 'Foot of Pride' evoked his then-recent album *New York*, the slinky groove of Dylan's take was very much a piece with the other songs recorded for *Infidels*. The song was part of the album sequence that Dylan put together with Mark Knopfler prior to removing the co-producer from the process. Some commentators wondered about Dylan's decision to drop the song, but this reaction paled in comparison to that surrounding the record's other eleventh-hour omission.

'Blind Willie McTell' became legendary almost as soon as *Infidels* was released without it. Questions came from journalists, and from people within Dylan's orbit – like Larry 'Ratso' Sloman, who had become friendly with Dylan while writing a book about the Rolling Thunder Revue. The narrative of a good album that could've been great had the artist not second-guessed himself, quickly became dogma among Dylan experts: a byproduct of the singer's own comments. Unlike his other cutting-room-floor masterwork from the early 1980s – 'Caribbean Wind' – the issues he cited with 'Blind Willie McTell' were not with the composition itself, so much as the process of committing it to tape. 'I didn't think I recorded it right,' he told Kurt Loder. If so, it wasn't for lack of trying – the song was recorded several times throughout the Power Station sessions, both with a full band and in an acoustic version with just Dylan on piano and Knopfler playing guitar.

The full band version of 'Blind Willie McTell' that was eventually released has many champions, but the acoustic rendition from the initial *The Bootleg Series* set is the purest expression of the Dylan/Knopfler collaboration. In the context of *Infidels'* studio polish, the simplicity of vocal, guitar and piano puts the essence of the song front and center. It also makes the decision to leave it off the record, more understandable. Assembling an album alternately preoccupied with the current state of the world and the world to come, Dylan may have decided an allegorical evocation of American history using the blues as its entry point, didn't fit.

The removal of a verse about slavery (from the lyrics posted on his official site, and from some live performances), indicates some rethinking of the piece. In any event, Bob Dylan has performed 'Blind Willie McTell' more often and more recently than any of the songs on *Infidels* itself. He began playing it in concert in 1997 – a few years after the reformed incarnation of The Band included the song on their 1993 album *Jericho* – and has played it as recently as 2017. A different version of 'Blind Willie McTell' appears on the upcoming *The Bootleg Series Vol. 16: Springtime In New York*, which includes numerous alternate takes and additional outtakes from *Infidels*.

Rather than touring, Dylan spent the remainder of the year playing informal jam sessions with younger musicians at his home studio. If these sessions were recorded, none have been released. However, like the punk and new wave shows he attended with his son Jesse, the jam sessions kept him engaged with the current music scene.

One of the main participants was drummer Charlie (sometimes called Chalo) Quintana. A founding member of Los Angeles band The Plugz – whose Spanish-language cover of 'Secret Agent Man' featured in the movie *Repo Man* – Quintana was already a veteran of the Southern California punk scene, and played in numerous bands, including Social Distortion, before his death in 2018. Asked about Dylan's view of the scene for a 2015 *Vulture* article, the drummer replied, 'Punk was just modern folk – a little political, a little sarcastic, telling real stories about the shit going down. Bob was into that.'

Quintana briefly joined the Never Ending Tour in 1992 and appeared in the music video for 'Sweetheart Like You', which was released as a single in December 1983. But his most significant contribution came the following year when he backed Dylan for one of the singer's most impressive televised performances.

1984: Standing on the Waters Casting Your Bread

When Bob Dylan was approached to perform on the popular US talk show *Late Night With David Letterman* for the first time, the commercially savvy move would've been to ask Mark Knopfler to appear with him. Knopfler might've passed in the wake of his ouster from the *Infidels* production, though, as an artist on the way up, it's also possible he would've seen the reciprocal benefits of appearing on television with a legend.

 Not surprisingly, after five years where Dylan was as likely to make a non-commercial choice as not, he took a rather more perverse path – Instead of performing with Letterman's studio band or any well-known musician acquaintances, Dylan brought a makeshift post-punk trio to accompany him for the March-1984 appearance. In addition to Charlie Quintana, this included the drummer's bandmate in Plugz bassist Tony Marsico, and guitarist J. J. Holliday: another participant in Dylan's home-studio jam sessions. The singer had apparently floated the idea of touring with some combination of these younger musicians, but according to Quintana, 'The Letterman show came out of nowhere.'

 Dylan's main concession to promotional niceties was playing two songs from his current album, even if he made a point of starting with 'Don't Start Me Talkin'': a 1955 R&B hit by Sonny Boy Williamson II, also covered by New York Dolls. After the requisite commercial break, the band played 'License To Kill' in an arrangement with style and tone calling to mind 1965's 'Queen Jane Approximately.' Whether deliberate or intuitive, the younger musicians' successful embrace of the *Highway 61 Revisited* sound two decades on made a strong case for how forward-looking Dylan's mid-1960s work had been and why he largely avoided the derision the punk generation directed at many of his contemporaries.

 'Jokerman' – the final song of the night, and apparently the only one the band had rehearsed consistently ahead of the show – was also revamped, turning its apocalyptic undertow into a crashing wave. A decade later, Dylan opened his set at the concert celebrating the 25th anniversary of the original Woodstock Festival, with the song. That rendition was very different from both the *Infidels* and *Letterman* show versions, making the song an excellent case study in how any iteration of a Bob Dylan song is just one way of hearing it.

 In retrospect, the combination of unexpected covers, sharp reworkings of Dylan's own repertoire, and musicians with something to prove, looks like a blueprint for what became the Never Ending Tour. Curiously, while all three musicians from the *Letterman* performance would have fit well in that setting, only Quintana worked with Dylan regularly after that. Marsico and Quintana continued to play together when The Plugz morphed into The Cruzados and signed a deal with Arista Records, while Holliday went on to perform and produce music with other artists, including various work for films and television.

While *Infidels* didn't fully restore Bob Dylan's commercial stature, it helped him regain a lot of ground. Unlike at certain points in his career, he was willing to acknowledge his celebrity and engage in some of the ephemera that went with it. A few weeks prior to the *Letterman* performance, he appeared at the 1984 Grammy Awards ceremony in Los Angeles, to present the award for the past year's best new song. Behind his sunglasses, he seemed nonplussed by fellow presenter Stevie Wonder's jokes about letting the audience choose the winner, but played along. 'We'd better do it the old-fashioned way,' Dylan quipped before the pair announced Sting's 'Every Breath You Take' as the winning composition.

Dylan also attempted to embrace the new reality of music video as a way to reach audiences. Though the famous clip for 'Subterranean Homesick Blues' predated MTV by more than a decade, his first effort in the MTV era turned out a bit ordinary. Despite having fairly ambitious ideas for 'Neighborhood Bully' – which he described in relation to the work of German filmmaker Rainer Werner Fassbinder – the singer was steered toward making a conventional performance video for the more accessible 'Sweetheart Like You.' Fortunately, when 'Jokerman' was picked as the next single, two of his associates from the Rolling Thunder Revue – 'Ratso' Sloman and George Lois – provided a path that was both literally and figuratively more artful.

George Lois had already established himself as one of America's premier ad designers by 1975, when he took an interest in the case of Rubin 'Hurricane' Carter. In spite of questionable police tactics and dubious evidence, in 1967, Carter was found guilty of murdering three people in a New Jersey bar. After reading the boxer's autobiography, Lois became convinced that Carter had been wrongfully convicted. A pair of skillfully designed ads in the *New York Times* sparked national attention for the case, and garnered the support of numerous celebrities, including Bob Dylan, who the ad-man met via 'Ratso' Sloman.

For the 'Jokerman' video, the pair pitched Dylan on using images of artwork and historical figures (himself included) to illustrate the lyrics, which were also displayed on-screen. Lois reputedly described the approach as 'Poetry right in your fuckin' face.' In addition to being more evocative than the typical MTV offering, it also minimized how much Dylan had to appear on camera. With the assistance of Hieronymus Bosch, Edvard Munch and other artists, he only needed to appear while singing the chorus. Though the singer remained skeptical of the format, the video was well-received and is a factor in why 'Jokerman' is so well-remembered.

When Dylan began a brief European tour in May 1984, 'Jokerman' kicked off the show. Though on the second night 'Highway 61 Revisited' displaced 'Jokerman' as the opener, the song remained a constant for the duration of the tour, along with 'I and I' and 'License To Kill' from the new album. The setlist otherwise focused on older material, with only 'Every Grain of Sand' and sometimes 'When You Gonna Wake Up?' representing the overtly-Christian albums with any regularity.

The emphasis on more-familiar material reflected the tour itinerary's emphasis on stadiums and other large-scale venues, as well as the input of promoter Bill Graham. Regardless of whether Dylan shared Graham's lean toward commercial considerations over artistic ones, as with the Grammy Awards appearance earlier in the year, he played along.

The arena-rock sensibility didn't just influence the song selection, but also the musicians selected to play them. Even if Mick Taylor hadn't contributed so much to *Infidels*, he would've been a sensible candidate due to his pedigree as a former member of The Rolling Stones. Former Faces keyboardist Ian McLagan fit this mold as well. Bass player Gregg Sutton was less well-known but still had an impressive background that included several years as comedian Andy Kaufman's musical director. Of the younger musicians Dylan enjoyed jamming with, Charlie Quintana was apparently the only one considered for this group, but was passed over in favor of Colin Allen who had played in John Mayall and The Bluesbreakers with Mick Taylor.

While many perceived *Infidels* as a break with the born-again period, the real shift in Dylan's work became apparent on the 1984 tour. For all that the new album's songs reframed his preoccupations, the concerns themselves remained very much the same (and continue to be). However, unlike the 1979-1981 period when the band that articulated his songs in concert were also the people recording them in the studio, as the decade progressed, recording-artist and performer became increasingly distinct roles for Dylan. If he had a stable band to record with, that ensemble generally wouldn't transfer to the stage, and vice versa.

Despite a rough start at the initial 1984 tour show in Italy, the group of musicians playing with Dylan turned out to be a very good match. Even with setlists that leaned heavily on his 1960s classics, the band didn't treat the songs as exercises in nostalgia. 'All Along the Watchtower' and 'Tombstone Blues' – the latter regularly performed with tour mate Carlos Santana – were tangible reminders that Dylan's evangelical fervor extended much further back than *Slow Train Coming*. Interviewed by Mick Brown of the *Sunday Times* ahead of July shows in the United Kingdom, Dylan made it clear that he saw the tour as more than a trip down memory lane: 'This term 'nostalgia', it's just another way people have of dealing with you and putting you some place they think they understand. It's just another label.'

Bill Graham, however, had no problem with that label, at least based on his decision to book Joan Baez for several dates early in the tour. Unbeknownst to Dylan, the promoter had assured Baez that, in addition to her own set, she'd perform some songs with the headliner. Presumably, Graham envisioned a callback to the Rolling Thunder Revue – or at least to the 1982 Peace Sunday concert – but didn't reckon with Dylan's reluctance to go down that path again, not to mention the contentious dynamic of he and Baez's post-relationship relationship. Television news footage from the 3 June Hamburg concert showed him none too happy to have Baez draping her arm around him during a stilted rendition of 'Blowin' in the Wind', and she soon left the tour.

The conviction Dylan expressed elsewhere in the *Sunday Times* interview, that 'None of the songs I've written has really dated', took melodic form at the next night's performance, in Rotterdam. While the lyrics for the original release of 'Tangled Up In Blue' represented one of his best narratives, they'd been a moving target since the recording sessions for *Blood on the Tracks*. Subsequent live performances featured various alterations to the song's specifics – such as the nature of the book being read from, and changing certain verses from first-person to third-person – but kept the overall story consistent. The 1984 iteration kept many of the specifics, but used them as the building blocks for an entirely new – and more complex – story. 'I wanted to defy time, so that the story took place in the present and the past at the same time,' he told Bill Flanagan. 'When you look at a painting, you can see any part of it or see all of it together. I wanted that song to be like a painting.' The degree of change became obvious in the second verse, which dealt with the main female character's failed marriage. Instead of recounting that 'She was

From 1988 to 2019, Dylan played more than 3,000 concerts on the so-called Never Ending Tour. (*Alamy*)

Left: Acclaimed artist Tony Wright's design for the cover of *Saved* was inspired by a vision Dylan had. (*Columbia*)

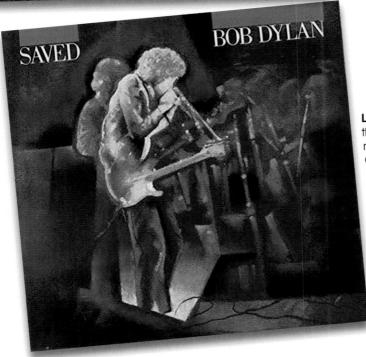

Left: To downplay the album's religious content, Columbia Records later replaced the original cover with a less provocative design. (*Columbia*)

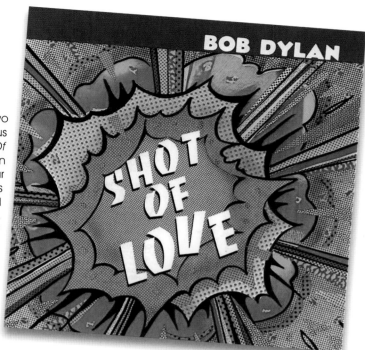

Right: After two explicitly religious albums, *Shot Of Love* found Dylan integrating secular preoccupations with his spiritual concerns. (*Columbia*)

Right: Seen by many fans as a return to form, *Infidels* nevertheless displayed a similarly apocalyptic mindset. (*Columbia*)

Left: The 1980 Grammy Award for 'Gotta Serve Somebody' was Dylan's first, and the only one for over a decade. (*Recording Academy*)

Right: Dylan's 1981 European tour mixed fan favorites like 'Mr. Tambourine Man' with recent religious work such as 'In the Garden'.

Left: Dylan performing the *Infidels'* closing track 'Don't Fall Apart on Me Tonight', which has been covered by multiple artists. (*Columbia*)

Right: Bob Dylan's working relationship with Mark Knopfler on *Infidels* became complicated but still yielded one of the singer's most compelling albums. (*Columbia*)

Left: Dylan appeared at the Philadelphia show of Live Aid as the final act before the concert's all-star finale.

Right: Dylan passed on a reunion with Peter, Paul and Mary in favor of Rolling Stones' Keith Richards and Ron Wood.

Left: Dylan's Live Aid performance was poorly received, but his on-stage remarks inspired Farm Aid (pictured here) – a benefit for struggling US farmers.

Right: Farm Aid was Dylan's final live performance of 1985 – and by far his most successful.

Left: Dylan and Tom Petty and the Heartbreakers enjoyed playing at Farm Aid so much they decided to tour together.

Right: The rock-star aspect of Dylan's public persona was frequently on display during the True Confessions Tour.

Left: Dylan appeared at the 1986 Farm Aid concert via satellite during the US leg of the tour.

Right: When Bob Dylan made himself available to reporters, they never knew which Dylan they were going to get. He's pictured here being interviewed with Neil Young.

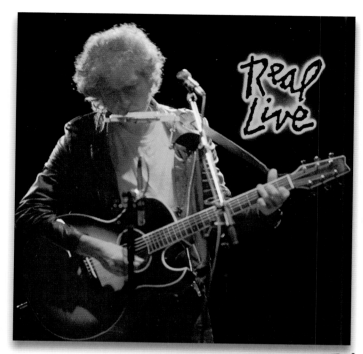

Left: *Real Live* documented Dylan's 1984 European tour featuring guitarist Mick Taylor. *(Columbia)*

Left: Both fans and critics were surprised by *Empire Burlesque's* embrace of synthesizers and other studio enhancements. *(Columbia)*

Right: Though *Knocked Out Loaded* was released during the True Confessions Tour, Dylan pretty much ignored the album in those shows. (*Columbia*)

Right: Largely seen as a low point in Dylan's career, *Down in the Groove* nonetheless includes several worthwhile performances. (*Columbia*)

Left: 1987's *Hearts of Fire* movie quickly disappeared from UK theatres and was released straight-to-video in the US. (*Warner Brothers*)

Right: A cover of John Hiatt's 'The Usual' for the soundtrack was one of the few highlights of the film. (*Columbia*)

Right: Dylan leaned into life imitating art when he agreed to play aging rock star Billy Parker in *Hearts of Fire*. (*Warner Brothers*)

Left: The movie's failure didn't help co-star Fiona Flanagan's ambitions to become a pop star. (*Warner Brothers*)

Right: The film's other lead, Rupert Everett, went on to have a successful film and television career. (*Warner Brothers*)

Left: The concert film *Hard to Handle* is the only officially released recording from the True Confessions Tour. (*HBO*)

Right: Backed by one of the world's best rock bands, Dylan gave raucous performances of classics such as 'Like a Rolling Stone'.

Left: The 1986 shows were followed in 1987 by a series of concerts in Israel and Europe.

Right: Bob Dylan's 1987 tour with the Grateful Dead came as the Dead's popularity was rising and his own was sinking. (*Sony*)

Left: Working with the Grateful Dead pushed the singer to play a broader selection of songs than on other recent tours.

Right: Dylan remained friends with Dead guitarist Jerry Garcia until Garcia's death in 1995.

Left: The culmination of a series of happy accidents, *The Traveling Wilburys Volume 1* was a huge success in 1988. (*Wilbury*)

Above: The Wilburys were the rare 'super group' where the quality of the musical output matched the members' celebrity.

Right: Working with U2 producer Daniel Lanois, Bob Dylan ended the 1980s with an understated masterpiece in 1989's *Oh Mercy*. (*Columbia*)

Left: The music video for 'Political World' was directed by singer and Farm Aid co-founder John Mellencamp. (*Columbia*)

Right: 'Everything Is Broken' was among the first songs from *Oh Mercy* that Dylan played in concert. (*Columbia*)

Left: Bob Dylan decided to start telling his own story in the 2004 release *Chronicles Volume One*. (*Simon & Schuster*)

Right: Among the many biographies of the singer, *Down the Highway* was noteworthy for its revelations about his personal life. (*Doubleday*)

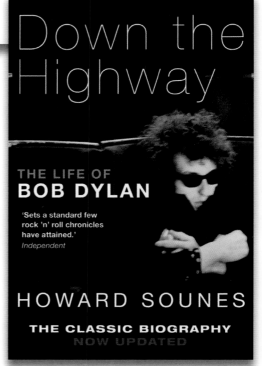

married when we first met / Soon to be divorced', the telling took a more dynamic turn:

> She was married when they first met
> To a man four times her age
> He left her penniless in a state of regret
> It was time to bust out of the cage

The payoff is even richer. The original release's narrator observes that 'We always did feel the same / We just saw it from a different point of view.' In the 1984 rendition, star-crossed romance gave way to a love triangle – though, once again, happiness proves elusive for all involved:

> Me, I'm still heading towards the sun
> Trying to stay out of the joint
> We always did love the very same one
> We just saw her from a different point of view
> Tangled up in blue

Dylan's efforts to repudiate the nostalgia label, extended to performing 'Enough Is Enough' – one of several new songs rehearsed during the tour, and the only one to make it to the stage. Performed solely in the tour's later shows and apparently never attempted in the studio, its so-so quality calls to mind the compositions that were performed on the *Shot of Love* tour but never revisited in other settings. That said, 'Enough Is Enough' – which recently appeared on a *Bootleg Series* release – played to the touring band's strengths, and demonstrated Dylan's confidence about being an artist with a future as well as an illustrious past.

With the reputation Dylan had forged in that past, it was inevitable that other artists would welcome the chance to join him on stage when the tour reached the United Kingdom. Guests for the encore at Wembley Stadium included Eric Clapton, Chrissie Hynde of The Pretenders and Van Morrison. Morrison shared lead vocals with Dylan on 'It's All Over Now Baby Blue', and repeated the performance for the tour's final show at Slane Castle in Ireland, where Morrison's own song 'Tupelo Honey' was added to the setlist. U2 singer Bono – who interviewed Dylan for Irish music magazine *Hot Press* – joined in for a passionate rendition of 'Blowin' in the Wind' that closed the show and tour. The most honest moment in the interview – which had subjects ranging from Ireland's musical tradition and recording technology, to chess – came when Dylan admitted, 'I wanna piss people off once in a while.' Though *Real Live* – the concert album drawn from the shows in Britain and Ireland – didn't necessarily piss fans off, neither did it really excite them. In spite of some good performances, solid song selection and the inclusion of the rewritten 'Tangled Up In Blue,' the record fell short of the Top 40 in both the US and UK.

Real Live (1984)

Personnel:
Bob Dylan: vocals, guitar and harmonica
Mick Taylor: guitar
Ian McLagan: keyboards
Greg Sutton: bass
Colin Allen: drums
Carlos Santana: additional guitar ('Tombstone Blues')
Prodicer: Glyn Johns
Release date: 26 November 1984
Chart places: US: 115, UK: 54
Running time: 50:15
All songs written by Bob Dylan.

Side One: 1. 'Highway 61 Revisited' 2. 'Maggie's Farm' 3. 'I And I' 4. 'License To Kill' 5. 'It Ain't Me'
Side Two: 1. 'Tangled Up In Blue' 2. 'Masters of War' 3. 'Ballad of a Thin Man' 4. 'Girl From the North Country' 10. 'Tombstone Blues'

The muted reception of *Real Live* seems less a function of its quality, than the perception of being largely inessential. *Before the Flood*'s documenting of Dylan's 1974 concerts with The Band notwithstanding, the live albums he released in close proximity to their respective tours, generally fit this description. Aside from the rewrite of 'Tangled Up in Blue', and the unavoidable spark of hearing 'Maggie's Farm' played on one of England's biggest stages during Margaret Thatcher's tenure as Prime Minister, the collection is solid but not necessarily revelatory in the way some of the *Bootleg Series* releases have been. In any case, by the time *Real Live* was released, Dylan had already moved on.

Shortly after the tour concluded, he began working on his next album at a pair of New York studios. Despite telling Kurt Loder that spring that he expected to record more songs with just guitar and harmonica as accompaniment, there was instead a cast of characters, featuring session drummer Anton Fig, and another Rolling Stones guitarist: Ron Wood. Dylan worked on new compositions, and revisited 'Clean Cut Kid': a piece originally written for *Infidels*. Among the new songs was 'Go 'Way Little Boy,' which was given to Lone Justice – an up-and-coming Los Angeles band signed to Geffen Records: where Dylan's sometime-girlfriend Carole Childs worked in the A&R department. He and Ron Wood recorded the song with Lone Justice, though a different take was ultimately released as the B-side of their first single, 'Sweet, Sweet Baby (I'm Falling).'

Another new talent that Dylan embraced came into his orbit via Ron Wood. Though still a teenager, Texas-born guitarist Charlie Sexton had been working professionally for a few years already when he played with Wood on a song for the soundtrack to the movie *The Wild Life*. Wood introduced Sexton to Keith Richards as well as Dylan. Sexton flirted with stardom the following year, thanks to his Top-20 single 'Beat's So Lonely' and the Keith-Forsey-produced album *Pictures For Pleasure*. This led to Sexton opening for David Bowie on some shows of his 1987 Glass Spider Tour, more Sexton solo albums and some with other artists, and multiple tenures with Dylan on the Never Ending Tour.

In November and December, Dylan resumed work on his own new record, this time in Los Angeles with musicians such as Lone Justice drummer Don Heffington. Only two of the new songs were ultimately released. But one of them – then known as 'New Danville Girl': a collaboration with playwright Sam Shepard – is among Dylan's most ambitious. However, with his working methods shifting from recording an album's worth of material in a concise time frame, to sporadic sessions over many months, it would be over a year until fans finally heard it.

1985: Until I Can Think My Way Out

Having finished his 1984 tour in Ireland, it seems strangely fitting that a scruffy Irish rock singer with a career trending in the wrong direction exerted an outsized influence on how Bob Dylan spent the following year. Dylan wasn't the only pop music figure caught up in the wave of social consciousness unleashed by Boomtown Rats singer Bob Geldof's charity project Band Aid and its worldwide hit 'Do They Know It's Christmas?' However, Dylan had a rather-more-complicated engagement with its international impact than most other well-known musicians.

The first stage came on 28 January when Dylan joined Michael Jackson, Lionel Richie and a couple of dozen other stars at A&M Recording Studios in Hollywood to record the American response to 'Do They Know It's Christmas?': 'We Are the World'. With many of the performers coming to the recording session straight from the American Music Awards ceremony, it's not surprising that the end result turned out to be somewhat self-congratulatory. In that context, it seems likely that Dylan was recruited out of a desire to give the undertaking cultural legitimacy, rather than out of any aesthetic or commercial considerations. Based on the footage of him rehearsing his vocals, and his self-deprecating comments made after the final take, the recording doesn't seem to have been especially enjoyable for him. That said, he gave an impassioned performance – albeit one that reinforced stereotypes about his singing voice – and whatever the song's artistic shortcomings, the money raised for famine relief helped a great many people.

As for his own work, Dylan returned to Los Angeles' Cherokee Studios to record several more new songs before returning to New York's Power Station in February to work on the remainder of the album. In keeping with the shifting locations, the singer utilized a rotating variety of session musicians. This included most of Tom Petty's band The Heartbreakers, and previous collaborators like Jim Keltner, Sly Dunbar and Robbie Shakespeare.

In their interview the previous year, Kurt Loder asked Dylan about his latest work. His response was surprisingly telling:

I just write 'em as they come, you know? They're not about anything different than what I've ever written about, but they're probably put together in a way that other ones aren't put together. So it might seem like somethin' new. I don't think I've found any new chords or new progressions, or any new words that haven't been said before. I think they're pretty much all the same old thing, just kinda reworked.

Reworking was the defining trait of Bob Dylan's mid-1980s releases. Whether rewriting previously recorded songs, adding new instrumental tracks to existing takes or recording backing tracks with the intention of filling in the lyrics later, this period was the furthest he diverged from his earlier working methods. In spite of these less organic origins, the first album that emerged from this process – *Empire Burlesque* – turned out to be quite cohesive overall. At the same time, it's an album of musical and lyrical contrasts – opening with the playful wordplay and sleek production of 'Tight Connection to My Heart', and closing with the earnest solo performance of 'Dark Eyes.'

Like *Infidels*, *Empire Burlesque* represented an effort to sound contemporary while remaining creatively faithful. However, even allowing for his dismissal of Mark Knopfler as co-producer in 1983, Dylan took a more rambling approach here than on *Infidels*. It was only after recording the majority of the album that he brought in producer Arthur Baker to help him finish it.

Baker – who was himself a Dylan fan – had a background in soul and dance music, and had worked as a DJ in clubs before branching into record production. His early production work included hip-hop records such as Afrika Bambaataa's 1982 single 'Planet Rock' and New Order's early hit 'Confusion,' both of which Baker co-wrote. He acquired further notoriety for his dance remixes of hits by Cyndi Lauper, Hall & Oates, and even Bruce Springsteen. Though not especially dance-oriented, *Empire Burlesque* reflects Baker's affinity for studio technology, and in a 1986 *Rolling Stone* interview, Dylan credited him with making the disparate tracks 'sound like a record.'

That sound factored into many reviews of *Empire Burlesque*, which were generally positive at the outset. In his full-page review for *Time* magazine, journalist and Martin-Scorsese-collaborator Jay Cocks likened Baker's studio acumen to that of a virtuoso musician. Cocks acknowledged that the sound was 'startling, an unexpected flash-forward', praising the dramatic qualities of the underlying songs, judging the album as 'a tentative triumph.'

Village Voice critic Robert Christgau also acknowledged the quality of the songs, calling the record Dylan's best since *Blood on the Tracks* – albeit with the caveat, 'I wish that was a bigger compliment.' Christgau was more pointed than most about the record's production; though his comments were more about outside perceptions than the music itself. The critic described outside references to the album as 'Disco Dylan,' as proof that 'His die-hard fans are even more alienated from current music than he is.' Dylan wasn't the only veteran artist to embrace 1980s production techniques that now sound dated, but – relative to his earlier records – those approaches seemed more incongruous than they did for someone like Lou Reed. As a result, some of the reactions to the album's electronic enhancements were over the top – exemplified by biographer Clinton Heylin's suggestion that fans need 'to file it with their New Order collections.'

Despite reviews from *Rolling Stone*, the *New York Times* and others asserting a return to form, fans remained largely unconvinced. Like *Shot of Love*, *Empire Burlesque* peaked at number 33 on the *Billboard* album chart, and became the first Bob Dylan album since the mid-1970s to miss the UK Top 10. Whatever one thinks about the quality of the songs or production and whether one aspect undercut the other, the album's commercial shortfall did not reflect a lack of effort on the singer's part.

Empire Burlesque (1985)

Personnel:

1.'Tight Connection to My Heart (Has Anybody Seen My Love)'
Bob Dylan: keyboards and vocal – Mick Taylor: guitar – Ted Perlman: guitar – Sly Dunbar: drums – Robbie Shakespeare: bass – Richard Scher: synthesizer – Carolyn Dennis, Queen Esther Marrow and Peggi Blu: backing vocals

2. 'Seeing The Real You At Last'
Bob Dylan: guitar and vocal – Mike Campbell: guitar – Benmont Tench: keyboards – Don Heffington: drums – Bob Glaub: bass – Bashiri Johnson: percussion – Chops: horns – David Watson: saxophone

3. 'I'll Remember You'
Bob Dylan: piano and vocal – Madelyn Quebec: vocal – Mike Campbell: guitar – Howie Epstein: bass – Jim Keltner: drums

4. 'Clean Cut Kid'
Bob Dylan: vocal, guitar – Ron Wood: guitar – Benmont Tench: piano – John Paris: bass – Anton Fig: drums – Carolyn Dennis, Queen Esther Marrow and Peggi Blu: backing vocals

5. 'Never Gonna Be the Same Again'
Bob Dylan: keyboards and vocal – Carolyn Dennis: vocal – Syd McGuiness: guitar
– Alan Clark: synthesizer – Richard Scher: synthesizer – Robbie Shakespeare: bass
– Sly Dunbar: drums – Queen Esther Marrow, Peggi Blu and Debra Byrd: backing
vocals

6. 'Trust Yourself'
Bob Dylan: guitar and vocal – Madelyn Quebec: vocal – Mike Campbell: guitar
– Benmont Tench: keyboards – Robbie Shakespeare: bass – Jim Keltner: drums –
Queen Esther Marrow, Debra Byrd and Carolyn Dennis: backing vocals

7. 'Emotionally Yours'
Bob Dylan: piano and vocal – Mike Campbell: guitar – Jim Keltner: drums – Howie
Epstein: bass – Benmont Tench: organ – Richard Scher: synth horns

8. 'When the Night Comes Falling From the Sky'
Bob Dylan: guitar and vocal – Madelyn Quebec: vocal – Sly Dunbar: drums –
Robbie Shakespeare: bass – Al Kooper: rhythm guitar – Stuart Kimball: electric
guitar – Bashiri Johnson: percussion – Richard Scher: synthesizer – Urban Blight
Horns: horns

9. 'Something's Burning Baby'
Bob Dylan: vocal – Madelyn Quebec: vocal – Ira Ingber: guitar – Vince
Melamed: synthesizer –Don Heffington: drums – Robbie Shakespeare: bass –
Richard Scher: synthesizer

10. 'Dark Eyes'
Bob Dylan: vocal, guitar and harmonica – Remix: Arthur Baker – Producer: Bob
Dylan (Uncredited) – Recording and mix engineer: Josh Abbey

Release date: 8 June 1985
Chart places: US: 33, UK: 11
Running Time: 46:24
All songs written by Bob Dylan.

One of Bob Dylan's most distinctive album openers, 'Tight Connection
to My Heart (Has Anybody Seen My Love)' establishes the mood
instantly, juxtaposing gospel singers against synthesizers and a rhythm
that's simultaneously inviting and insistent. The song started life as

'Someone's Got A Hold Of My Heart' and was recorded at the *Infidels* sessions. That song – multiple takes of which have been released via *The Bootleg Series* – remains the foundation of 'Tight Connection To My Heart.' Dylan retained Sly and Robbie's rhythm track and Mick Taylor's guitar part, but replaced other instrumental parts and added the backing singers. The return of the gospel vocalists – after being absent (Clydie King aside) since *Shot of Love* – in itself gave the revamped track a very different feel. But the biggest divergence came in the lyrics. Comparing the *Bootleg Series* releases of the song makes an interesting case study in how subtle individually minor edits can shift the overall feel. After a line in which 'They're beating the devil out of a guy who's wearing a powder-blue wig,' the two songs convey very different scenes. In the earlier version, the narrator recounts:

I been to Babylon
I gotta confess
I could still hear the voice crying in the wilderness

On *Empire Burlesque*, Dylan focuses on the victim. By turning the song outward, he ultimately makes it feel more personal:

Later he'll be shot
For resisting arrest
I can still hear his voice crying in the wilderness

In keeping with the aphorism that good artists borrow but great artists steal, some of the most memorable lyrics were appropriated from movies and television programs. Aside from references to a Bogart film, Dylan puts himself in Captain Kirk's frame of mind with the line, 'I'll go along with the charade until I can think my way out'. This trait made the song a natural choice for his most cinematic effort in the music video realm – executed with the help of filmmaker Paul Schrader.

The video was shot in Tokyo, where Schrader had recently directed *Mishima: A Life in Four Chapters*: an unconventional biographical film about writer Yukio Mishima. Unfortunately, despite being visually striking and hinting at a compelling narrative, the *Mishima*-meets-*Miami-Vice* result satisfied neither Dylan nor the director. Dylan later admitted that his hope that working with someone who actually made movies would yield a satisfying video, was misplaced; while Schrader offered self-deprecating commentary at a June-1985 press conference that followed a screening of both *Mishima* and the music video:

> That was a little piece of eye candy I shot in Tokyo about six weeks ago; a little *hors d'oeuvre*. It means as little as it looks like it means. I just did it to keep my hand in, to save me from falling into unemployment.

The intervening years did not diminish the director's disappointment. Reflecting on the experience in a 2018 interview, he recalled telling Dylan, 'Bob, if you ever hear I'm doing another music video, take me out in the backyard and hose me down'. Nevertheless, Schrader maintained great respect for Dylan as an artist. When Schrader made his 1992 film *Light Sleeper*, he sought to use five of Dylan's *Empire Burlesque* songs to serve as an additional voice for the main character (played by Willem Defoe). However, as he told an interviewer for the magazine *Filmmaker*, that plan had to be abandoned after discussions with Dylan revealed that 'I didn't want the songs he wanted to give me, and he didn't want to give me the songs I wanted.'

'Seeing The Real You At Last' continues the album's focus on challenging relationships, with a song that resides in the space between 'Positively 4th Street' and *Blood on the Tracks*. Part kiss-off and part reminiscence, it was a regular part of Dylan's shows with Tom Petty and The Heartbreakers: two of whom – Mike Campbell and Benmont Tench – played on the album version.

Before performing it at one of the shows, Dylan told the audience, 'I've written a lot of songs that can be taken more ways than one. It just happens that way accidentally. Well, here's a song that can't be taken but one way.' Based on the series of issues the song catalogs, it would be hard to argue with that assessment:

> Well, I have had some rotten nights
> Didn't think that they would pass
> I'm just thankful and grateful
> To be seeing the real you at last

The ballad 'I'll Remember You' was another song featuring studio contributions from The Heartbreakers, that Dylan also first played live with the group. The recording also reunited him with two veterans of his 1979-1981 ensemble: drummer Jim Keltner and vocalist Madelyn Quebec.

While the lyrics – with their imagery of faded roses and 'rain blowing in your hair' – read like an ode to a lost love, the song's closest kindred in mood and style is *Shot of Love*'s 'Lenny Bruce.'

Empire Burlesque changes gear quickly with 'Clean Cut Kid' – a song that tells the story of an ordinary kid whose life takes a bitter turn when sent 'to a napalm health spa to shape up'. Contrasting the young man's life before and after Vietnam, culminates in a simple but rather damning observation:

> Well, everybody's asking why he couldn't adjust
> All he ever wanted was somebody to trust

Presenting the young man's fate as symbolizing a wholesale betrayal of the American Dream, may be why Robert Christgau described it as 'the toughest Vietnam vet song yet.' It's unclear how seriously any of the takes recorded during the *Infidels* sessions were considered for that album, but using an individual to make a broader point is far more effective than most of the earlier record's dispatches on the state of the world.

Between *Infidels* and *Empire Burlesque*, Los Angeles band Carla Olson and The Textones recorded 'Clean Cut Kid' for their debut album *Midnight Mission*, with fellow Dylan interpreter Ry Cooder also playing on the track. In an interesting example of Dylan's worlds colliding, the song was given to Olson as a token of gratitude for appearing in the 'Sweetheart Like You' video, for which she learned Mick Taylor's guitar part in order to simulate it convincingly on screen. This in turn led to her collaborating with the former Rolling Stone on several future projects.

After starting with a strong sequence of songs, the first side closes with one of the album's weaker tracks. 'Never Gonna Be The Same Again' is both musically and lyrically slight, and Dylan's vocal does nothing to elevate it. Though the backing singers make a solid effort, the synthesizer parts distract from the melody. Perhaps the intention was to differentiate this song from 'I'll Remember You,' but a more spare arrangement would've fit the song better.

Conversely, the 1980s-style enhancements suit the second side's opening track 'Trust Yourself' quite well. Drummer Jim Keltner was reportedly disappointed that electronics augmented his performance, but the track's fusion of musical sensibilities is among the album's most successful – with Robbie Shakespeare, Mike Campbell and Benmont Tench all playing their part. The female backing singers' contribution reveals the song's soul as a kind of commentary on the most famous song from Dylan's Christian albums. Having previously used a crack studio band and gospel singers to admonish listeners that they're 'gonna have to serve somebody,' Dylan now advised them to 'Trust yourself to do what's right and not be second-guessed.' As on *Infidels*, he hadn't abandoned religious convictions in his music, but rather reframed their presentation. Like many of the best songs from that period, the 'Trust Yourself' lyric incorporates biblical references organically, so that the 'land of wolves and thieves' sounds like the voice of experience instead of something heard secondhand.

'Emotionally Yours' cuts the deepest of all the *Empire Burlesque* love songs. Where 'Never Gonna Be The Same Again' strains to convey a life profoundly changed by love, 'Emotionally Yours' is one of Dylan's most perfect romantic declarations.

It's like my whole life never happened
When I see you, it's as if I never had a thought
I know this dream, it might be crazy
But it's the only one I got

'Emotionally Yours' had a well-deserved second life when soul band The O'Jays recorded it for their 1991 album of the same name. Released as a single, it reached number 5 on the US R&B chart, and helped the album earn a Gold record certification.

While Bob Dylan was not at this point producing new American standards the way he had earlier in his career – and wouldn't again until 1997's 'Make You Feel My Love' – another *Empire Burlesque* song was covered soon after the album's release. 'When the Night Comes Falling From the Sky' appeared performed by The Jeff Healey Band on the soundtrack to the 1989 Patrick Swayze movie *Road House*.

Dylan had recorded the song twice during the *Empire Burlesque* sessions, and the two approaches make for an interesting comparison. On the first recording, he was accompanied by Roy Bittan and Steve Van Zandt from Bruce Springsteen's E Street Band. At least one account holds that Dylan felt this version sounded too much like Springsteen. Listening to the recording on the initial *Bootleg Series* set, the issue isn't so much that it sounds like Springsteen, as that it sounds like an anonymous piece of album rock. In any event, the singer decided to re-record it, keeping Sly and Robbie as the rhythm section, but otherwise featuring different musicians, including Al Kooper on guitar.

The synthesizers and other additions to the mix obviously aren't to everyone's taste, but like 'Trust Yourself,' the parts add up to a unique whole, especially with Dylan's more engaged vocal as a unifying force. More than any song on the album, 'When the Night Comes Falling From the Sky' continued the tradition of love-in-the-end-times compositions like 'Caribbean Wind', though with more direct lyrics than that earlier song.

> I saw thousands who could have overcome the darkness
> For the love of a lousy buck, I've watched them die
> Stick around, baby, were not through
> Don't look for me, I'll see you
> When the Night Comes Falling From the Sky

Despite decidedly cinematic lyrics, Dylan opted for a fairly straightforward performance video, made with Dave Stewart from Eurythmics. In tandem with an interlinked video for 'Emotionally Yours', there's a modest narrative thread, but it's much more submerged than the song warrants. Cutting some of the verses to keep the video under five minutes long did the song no favors either. While not the singer's finest attempted epic of the decade, it benefits from its lyric's collective impact.

The penultimate song – 'Something's Burning Baby' – likewise walks the line between personal and universal Armageddon, even if the latter is mainly implied. The 'man going 'round calling names' in the final verse while 'something's in flames', contrasts sharply with the promises of salvation earlier in the song.

> You can't live by bread alone, you won't be satisfied
> You can't roll away the stone if your hands are tied

'Something's Burning Baby' is one of the songs Paul Schrader wanted to use for *Light Sleeper*, and the martial drum rhythm and slow build would've worked well in the context of the moody thriller. Those elements also would've made it a concert highlight, but it's the only *Empire Burlesque* song Dylan never played on stage.

Live performances of the album's closing track 'Dark Eyes' have been similarly elusive. After one interrupted attempt in 1986, he didn't perform the song again until 1995 when he sang it as a duet with Patti Smith at several shows on the Never Ending Tour. Performed solo on the album –

Dylan accompanied only by his own guitar and harmonica – 'Dark Eyes' was written at the end of the album sessions, at the urging of Arthur Baker. Baker's sense that the album should end with an acoustic number, apparently tapped into the singer's own thinking. In his 2004 memoir *Chronicles: Volume One*, Dylan recounted the encounter that inspired the song. Getting off the elevator at his New York hotel, he saw a dark-eyed call girl in the hallway. 'She had a beautifulness', he recalled, 'but not for this kind of world.'

Though Dylan didn't go on tour immediately after the album's release, his three live appearances that year were all momentous. 25 July saw his first and only live performance in the Soviet Union. At the invitation of Yevegeny Yevtushenko – a poet to whom Dylan was compared in the 1960s – he appeared in Moscow at an international celebration of poetry, sponsored by the Union of Soviet Writers. According to a *Washington Post* account of the event, the singer himself was unsure if his records had been officially released in the USSR; while others in attendance wondered if he could truly be considered a poet. This might account for the muted response to his renditions of 'A Hard Rain's a-Gonna Fall,' 'The Times They Are a-Changin' and 'Blowin' in the Wind.'

The Moscow event was the second time Dylan played 'Blowin' in the Wind' that month. The first – which came less than two weeks earlier – wasn't necessarily better-received, but certainly had greater impact. When Joan Baez kicked off the Philadelphia portion of the 13 July Live Aid concert, she proclaimed to the audience, 'This is your Woodstock'. As a practical matter, the 1985 event had many differences from its legendary ancestor – one of the most tangible being that Dylan actually performed at Live Aid. Aesthetically speaking, that performance turned out to be a bit shaky: especially 'Blowin' in the Wind.' Though the original plans called for him to appear with Peter, Paul and Mary, Dylan decided that Keith Richards and Ron Wood better fit his mood. Unfortunately, his place on the bill – immediately preceding the all-hands-on-deck performance of 'We Are the World' – meant that the stage monitors had been turned off to enable the group at large to practice the finale. This left the trio in front of the curtain, unable to hear themselves as they played.

If Joan Baez attempted to position Live Aid as a 1980s equivalent to the Woodstock festival, Bob Dylan had another idea, and perhaps greater cognizance of the biggest difference between the events. Despite how the 1969 festival unfolded, it started life as a commercial undertaking. Bob Geldof's intent in organizing Live Aid was charitable, and working in a similar spirit, Dylan ironically generated a bit of static when he made an unexpected proposal prior to his second song. Before playing 'When the Ship Comes In,' he related the hope that 'some of the money that's raised for the people in Africa, maybe they could just take a little bit of it – maybe one or two million maybe – and use it to, say, to pay the...pay the mortgages on some of the farms...the farmers here owe the banks.'

In his autobiography, Geldof derided Dylan's remarks as a 'complete lack of understanding of the issues raised by Live Aid' and 'a crass, stupid and nationalistic thing to say.' However, he also conceded that something good came of them.

Willie Nelson took Dylan's remarks to heart, and along with John Mellencamp and Neil Young, organized the September 1985 Farm Aid concert to help financially struggling farmers, and invited Dylan to perform. At Bill Graham's suggestion, Dylan asked Tom Petty and The Heartbreakers – who were scheduled to perform their own set at the event – to back him. After a week of rehearsals and a full soundcheck the night before, the Farm Aid performance was as tightly focused as the one at Live Aid had felt shambolic. The Farm Aid performance also stood out from other recent appearances by emphasizing songs from Dylan's latest album, though he fittingly concluded the set with 'Maggie's Farm.'

Dylan and Petty soon decided to tour together, and later in the year began rehearsals for shows in New Zealand, Australia and Japan. Dylan also continued working on new music at Dave Stewart's studio in London. In addition to his work with Annie Lennox as Eurythmics, by the mid-1980s, Stewart had branched out into writing and producing for others, including Tom Petty and Bob Geldof. While only one song has been released from the Dylan/Stewart sessions, the trip inspired an installment of the 2017 Sky Arts television series *Urban Myths – Bob Dylan: Knockin' on Dave's Door*.

The following month, Dylan could be heard speaking up for another social cause alongside Bruce Springsteen, Bono and many others as part of the ad hoc group Artists United Against Apartheid. The single 'Sun City' – written by Steve Van Zandt (who organized the effort) and produced by Van Zandt and Arthur Baker – didn't have the same commercial impact of songs like 'We Are the World'. It barely reached the US Top 40, but still raised a significant amount of money to support anti-apartheid projects. Beyond that, Van Zandt saw the record as a success for the attention it drew to Sun City – a luxury resort exploited by the apartheid regime to circumvent the United Nations' cultural boycott of South Africa. 'Our goal was to stop performers from going there,' he told *Rolling Stone* in 1989. 'And to this day, no major artists of any integrity have played Sun City.' While recent songs like 'Neighborhood Bully' and 'Union Sundown' suggested muddled politics on Dylan's part, the singer's involvement in projects like this and Farm Aid, showed that he still retained a fundamental sense of empathy.

At the end of 1985, as Bob Dylan looked to the future, his past was on prominent display via the November release of the 53-track box-set *Biograph*. This kind of career retrospective is ubiquitous now, but at the time was unusual and even celebrated by his record company with a gala event at New York's Whitney Museum of Art. Because it was intended for release a couple of years earlier, the set's most recent material came from *Shot of Love*. Nevertheless, with its mix of iconic songs and eighteen previously unreleased recordings (at least officially), it remains the finest single compilation of his work. More importantly for those who enjoy his work, *Biograph*'s success set the stage for the launch of the ongoing *Bootleg Series* several years later.

1986: Too Far From Shore

By many measures, the True Confessions Tour was a triumph for Bob Dylan. With Tom Petty and The Heartbreakers being a headline act in their own right, the shows were well-attended, allowing for a solid balance between art and commerce. Dylan having one of his best backing bands ever – capable of bringing both his new material and classics to life – hypothetically meant that virtually his entire songbook was open to him, along with a wide range of covers. One of the most commonly played was 'Lonesome Town' – frequently presented as a tribute to Ricky Nelson, who'd died in a plane crash on New Year's Eve 1985. Dylan admired the former teen-idol, who sang 'his songs calm and steady like he was in the middle of a storm' and made his version's of Dylan songs 'sound like he had written them himself'. Reflecting on the famous incident where an audience booed Nelson for not playing the songs they wanted to hear, Dylan observed, 'It turned out we did have a lot in common.'

In *Chronicles: Volume One*, Dylan revealed his own sense of disquiet about this period of his career. But in the moment, he appeared comfortable and confident. Before the tour started though, Dylan was called upon to fulfill his role as cultural icon again, albeit for another worthy purpose. In the early-1980s, Stevie Wonder was among the most vocal campaigners for a federal holiday in the United States to commemorate the birthday of civil rights icon Dr. Martin Luther King Jr. After more than a decade of stymied congressional efforts, President Reagan signed the bill into law in 1983, establishing the holiday, and the event was first observed on 20 January 1986. To mark the occasion, Wonder helped organize a celebratory concert at the John F. Kennedy Center for the Performing Arts in Washington, D.C. The show, which aired on NBC, was a benefit for the Martin Luther King Jr. Center for Nonviolent Social Change. Other performers included Peter, Paul and Mary and Diana Ross. Also appearing was Dylan, who had also performed at King's 1963 March on Washington. Having opted against performing 'Blowin' in the Wind' with Peter, Paul and Mary at Live Aid the year before, he joined them to sing the civil rights anthem at *this* show. They were joined by Stevie Wonder, whose own recording of the song had hit the US Top 10 and topped the R&B chart in 1966, also hitting the UK Top 40.

Little more than two weeks later, Dylan, Petty and The Heartbreakers opened their tour in Wellington, New Zealand. The concert nearly didn't happen when complaints about the group's loud and lengthy soundcheck at the open-air venue led the local government to consider withdrawing their permit.

Like the 1984 European tour, the setlist featured many of the 1960s Dylan classics that fans might consider obligatory; though, the inclusion of songs like 'Lenny Bruce' and 'In The Garden' meant that the Christian-oriented albums were more thoroughly represented this time around.

Unsurprisingly – considering the participation of several of the Heartbreakers in the studio – the band sounded highly engaged with the new *Empire Burlesque* songs. At the same time, the significance of Dylan's older work was not lost on his fellow musicians. Interviewed for a *Rolling Stone* article about the tour, guitarist Mike Campbell recalled the impression 'Like A Rolling Stone' had made on him when he first heard it: 'This is the first song I ever learned on the guitar,' he said. 'And here I am playing it with the person who wrote it.'

The gospel-style backing singers – now dubbed the Queens of Rhythm – were another important musical element in these shows. After a four-year absence from Dylan's concert performances, the singers were part of the Farm Aid performance, and remained a presence throughout the tour, with the lineup shifting occasionally for various reasons. For the shows in New Zealand, this included Debra Byrd, Queen Esther Marrow, Elisecia Wright and Madelyn Quebec. Quebec's daughter Carolyn Dennis had performed at Farm Aid, but was unavailable for these shows due to giving birth to Bob Dylan's sixth child – Desiree Gabrielle Dennis-Dylan – on 31 January. Carolyn Dennis and Dylan had been involved intermittently since the late-1970s. After a failed marriage on her part, and ongoing romantic entanglements on his, they resumed their relationship in the mid-1980s. Though Dylan married Dennis later in the year, and supported Desiree financially, the child's paternity was kept private until revealed in Howard Sounes' 2001 biography *Down the Highway: The Life of Bob Dylan*.

After a well-received concert in Auckland, the tour continued on to Sydney, Australia, where Bob Dylan and The Heartbreakers recorded one of their few studio collaborations. Produced by Tom Petty, 'Band of the Hand' – the title song for a largely forgotten action movie – could more accurately be called 'It's Hell Time, Man!' This line was repeated throughout the song, and was sometimes listed as its subtitle. Though neither the single nor the movie performed especially well following their April releases, the song was played at many of that summer's North American shows. It's unclear how much Dylan knew about the movie's plot – involving reformed juvenile delinquents taking on a Miami drug lord – when he was hired. Regardless, the end result has a tangible kick, thanks to The Heartbreakers, Queens of Rhythm, and also Stevie Nicks, who'd been traveling with the ensemble but didn't join them on stage until the second Sydney show. With their help, Dylan got a prime chance to paint a fiery portrait of earthly corruption and chaos.

> They kill people here who stand up for their rights
> The system's just too damned corrupt
> It's always the same, the name of the game
> Is who do you know higher up

The group played six shows in total at the Sydney Entertainment Centre, the last two of which were filmed for the HBO concert special *Hard To Handle*. Director Gillian Armstrong is better known for her dramatic work, but has also received acclaim for her documentaries. What stands out about *Hard To Handle*, is the way it reworks the running order from the original shows, to craft a concise portrait of Dylan's artistry.

The film begins with 'In the Garden' – the last song played before the encores – prefaced by a speech from Dylan about heroes: variations on which were customary during the tour. Before the band starts playing, he names a variety of contemporary figures some might see as heroes before declaring, 'I don't care nothing about none of those people. I have my own hero. I'm gonna sing it about my hero now.' Opening the film this way was a bold choice. Beyond being a fairly obscure song, 'In the Garden' also foregrounded the religious aspects of Dylan's work at a point where he'd seemingly put them aside in favor of embracing the role of rock star.

The rock star aspect gets its due with 'Like A Rolling Stone' and 'When the Night Comes Falling From the Sky,' but the song choice lets several facets come through. A pair of acoustic numbers – 'It's Alright Ma (I'm Only Bleeding)' and 'Girl From the North Country' – are a bit rough, but show that Dylan didn't need The Heartbreakers for his singing to be passionate. Next in the film, an impressive rendition of 'Lenny Bruce' makes the scope of the band's contribution – specially Benmont Tench's playing – obvious. The film is currently out of print, but could be a candidate for inclusion on a future *Bootleg Series* release.

Between the initial Sydney shows and the later ones filmed for HBO, the tour played three other cities in Australia. On 19 February – the night before the first of three shows in Melbourne – Dylan had another rock star moment. After Mark Knopfler joined the group for the encore at one of the Sydney shows, Dylan reciprocated by appearing with Dire Straits at one of their shows supporting their blockbuster album *Brothers in Arms*.

Among the alternate-universe iterations of Bob Dylan's career that fans love to ponder, one where he toured with Dire Straits in 1986 rather than Tom Petty and The Heartbreakers, is an interesting concept. As a practical matter, Dylan probably would've become disenchanted with Dire Straits' polished style before long, but based on the recording from the February show, it would have fostered some intriguing takes on his songs while it lasted. Though 'Knockin' on Heaven's Door' is the song that makes everyone raise their game where Dylan is concerned, the night's performance of 'License To Kill' seems more consequential. Playing something from *Infidels*, telegraphed rapprochement between Dylan and Knopfler in a way an older classic couldn't. The song provided a satisfying postscript to the events surrounding *Infidels*.

The first leg of the True Confessions Tour concluded with four shows in Japan. During the encores, Dylan and the band payed their respects to the host nation with an instrumental rendition of the 1961 hit 'Ue O Muite Arukō (known elsewhere as 'Sukiyaki') before their customary finale of 'Knockin' on Heaven's Door.' Not long after their return to the United States, they announced the tour's North American segment, which many fans had hoped for when the Australian dates were announced. Both lead singers were in good form at the press conference to announce the new shows. Attributing their collaboration to the money involved, Petty also noted the advantages of Dylan being the headliner: 'Your throat doesn't get nearly as sore, because Bob's doing most of the work.' Meanwhile, still fielding questions about his religious beliefs, Dylan noted, 'I'm only Jewish when I have to be'. Perhaps the most honest response came when Petty told reporters that he and Dylan decided to tour together because they 'just felt like it.'

However much Dylan felt like touring, he seemed somewhat less engaged in putting together a new album. His studio work from the past two years included a handful of songs in various stages of evolution, but he seemed unsure of what shape the rest of the album should take. *Rolling Stone* reporter Mikal Gilmore described inspired sessions with musicians such as T Bone Burnett and Al Kooper, where the sound was reminiscent of *Highway 61 Revisited*, but Dylan put that aside in favor of a hodgepodge of new and existing material. Among those disappointed by this decision, was Al Kooper, who eulogized the experience by saying, 'There was some really wonderful things cut at those sessions, but I don't think we'll ever hear 'em.'

The end result was *Knocked Out Loaded* – an album of disparate pieces, with a title seemingly chosen on the basis that Dylan just liked the sound of it. 'It doesn't really have a theme or purpose,' he told Gilmore. A quick look at the songwriting credits, emphasizes this point. Bookended by a loose rewrite of a song by a blues icon, and a fitful collaboration with an artist better known for their adult-contemporary hits, *Knocked Out Loaded* represents the peak of Dylan's uncertainty as a recording artist.

With this period's disconnect between Dylan as a recording artist and as a performer had started to manifest publicly on the 1984 tour, *Knocked Out Loaded* provided a lasting souvenir of this – at least, it did for the relatively few people who actually purchased the record. The singer's decision to play virtually nothing from the album on the tour that ostensibly provided the reason for releasing a new record in the first place, helped keep that record-buyer cohort small. This also positioned the album in a similar category as *Saved* – where reflexively negative views are intertwined with self-reinforcing conventional wisdom that keeps it in the lower end of rankings.

Listening to *Knocked Out Loaded* in the context of work from other veteran artists who found themselves struggling in one way or another in the 1980s, the 1984 David Bowie album *Tonight* – the polarizing follow-up to *Let's Dance* – comes to mind. Though not an exact comparison in commercial terms, the parallel of moving from embracing an uncharacteristic new sound to a collection of odds and ends assembled under less than ideal circumstances, holds. Not having an album's worth of new compositions ready, Bowie made up the difference by highlighting the work of artists he admired, such as Iggy Pop. Dylan did much the same, but with touchstones that went a bit further back. Both artists might've been better off fully embracing a *Pin Ups/Self Portrait* approach, making a full album recasting others' work in their own image, and saving their own songs for their next record. Though the end results in both cases are a bit slight (and occasionally embarrassing), neither *Tonight* nor *Knocked Out Loaded* deserves the full measure of derision they've received over the past few decades.

Knocked Out Loaded (1986)
Personnel:

1.'You Wanna Ramble' (Herman Parker Jr.)
Bob Dylan: guitar and vocals – T Bone Burnett: guitar – James Jamerson Jr.: bass – Al Kooper: keyboards – Raymond Lee Pounds: drums – Carolyn Dennis, Madelyn Quebec, Muffy Hendrix and Annette May Thomas: background vocals

2.'They Killed Him' (Kris Kristofferson)
Bob Dylan: guitar and vocals – Jack Sherman: guitar – Vito San Filippo: bass – Raymond Lee Pounds: drums – Al Kooper: keyboards – Steve Douglas: saxophone – Steve Madaio: trumpet: Carolyn Dennis, Madelyn Quebec, Muffy Hendrix and Annette May Thomas – background vocals: The Children's Choir – Damien Turnbough, Majason Bracey, Keyshawn Gwin, Crystal Pounds, Lara Firestone, Tiffany Wright, Chyna Wright, Angel Newell, Herbert Newell, Larry Mayhand, April Hendrix-Haberlan, Dewey B. Jones II, Modena Smith, Diana Smith and Maia Smith

3.'Driftin' Too Far From Shore'
Bob Dylan: keyboards and vocals: Ron Wood – guitar: Anton Fig: drums: John Paris – bass: Peggi Blu, Annette May Thomas, Madelyn Quebec, Carolyn Dennis and Muffy Hendrix – background vocals

4.'Precious Memories' (Arr. Bob Dylan)
Bob Dylan – guitar and vocals: Raymond Lee Pounds – drums: James Jamerson Jr. – bass: Larry Meyers – mandolin: Al Perkins – steel guitar: Milton Gabriel, Mike Berment and Brian Paris – steel drums: Queen Esther Marrow, Carolyn Dennis, Madelyn Quebec, Muffy Hendrix and Annette May Thomas – background vocals

5.'Maybe Someday'
Bob Dylan – guitar and vocals: Mike Campbell – guitar: Howie Epstein – bass: Don Heffington – drums: Steve Douglas – saxophone: Steve Madaio – trumpet: Annette May Thomas, Carolyn Dennis, Madelyn Quebec, Elisecia Wright, Queen Esther Marrow and Peggi Blu – background vocals

6.'Brownsville Girl' (Bob Dylan, Sam Shepard)
Bob Dylan – guitar and vocals: Don Heffington – drums:– Carl Sealove – bass: Vince Melamed – keyboards: Ira Ingber – guitar: Steve Douglas – saxophone: Steve Madaio – trumpet: Elisecia Wright, Queen Esther Marrow, Muffy Hendrix, Carolyn Dennis, Madelyn Quebec and Peggi Blu – background vocals

7.'Got My Mind Made Up' (Bob Dylan, Tom Petty)
Bob Dylan – vocals: Tom Petty – guitar: Mike Campbell – guitar: Benmont Tench
– keyboards: Stan Lynch – drums: Howie Epstein – bass: Philip Lyn Jones – conga:
Carolyn Dennis, Queen Esther Marrow, Eliseçia Wright and Madelyn Quebec –
background vocals

8.'Under Your Spell' (Bob Dylan, Carole Bayer Sager)
Bob Dylan – guitar and vocals: Dave Stewart – guitar: Clem Burke – drums: Patrick
Seymour – keyboards: John McKenzie – bass: Muffy Hendrix, Carolyn Dennis,
Queen Esther Marrow, Eliseçia Wright and Madelyn Quebec – background vocals

Producer: Bob Dylan
Engineers: Britt Bacon, Judy Feltus, Don Smith, George Tutko
Release date: US: 8 August 1986, UK: 14 July 1986
Chart places: US: 53, UK: 35
Running time: 35:18
Songs written by Bob Dylan, except as noted.

Compared to songs like 'Jokerman' or 'Tight Connection To My Heart,' 'You Wanna Ramble' is an unimpressive way to open an album. On the plus side, this loose rewrite of Junior Parker's 'I Wanna Ramble' starts *Knocked Out Loaded* on an agreeable note, and the band all sound like they're having fun. However, it sounds more like Dylan simply rolled tape during one of the cover songs he liked to play between takes of new songs and decided to put it on an album. That's more or less what happened with 'A Satisfied Mind' during the recording of *Saved*, but the earlier album's consistency of sound and subject matter made that potential tangent a perfect fit. Because *Knocked Out Loaded* is basically a collection of tangents, each piece has to stand on its own merits.

That metric is far kinder to some tracks than others, as Dylan's rendition of Kris Kristofferson's 'They Killed Him' attests. A tribute to Mahatma Ghandi, Dr. Martin Luther King Jr. and Jesus – three figures who died fighting for social change – 'They Killed Him' obviously has worthy subject matter. But *that* doesn't necessarily make it a worthwhile song. One imagines Kristofferson saw it as a successor to the oft-covered 1968 hit 'Abraham, Martin and John' – especially with the reference to 'the Brothers Kennedy' at the end of his version. Perhaps that's what attracted Dylan, who performed the earlier song on tour in 1980 and 1981. Regardless of whether it provided direct inspiration, 'Abraham, Martin and John' is a good point of comparison for how to execute this kind of song. Neither composition is particularly distinguished lyrically, but framing its portrait in personal terms enables the older one to sidestep sanctimony. In contrast, an overwhelming sense of piety in 'They Killed Him' is its undoing. The best and worst of Kristofferson's song is embodied in a single couplet. The line 'Just another holy man who dared to make a stand' is compelling, but following it with the exclamation 'My God, they killed him,' alternately feels like self-parody or an insult to the listener's intelligence.

Though Dylan's rendition of 'They Killed Him' preceded Kristofferson's own – released later that year on his album *Repossessed* – it wasn't the first. Johnny Cash recorded a version in 1984. Dylan might've been inspired to record the song after hearing Kristofferson play it at Farm Aid, but he probably heard Cash's recording also. Like Bob's version, Cash's also featured an ill-advised children's choir. Something about the song invites lapses of taste – a trait embodied by Kristofferson's music video, which included an image of John Lennon amid the other figures. The other uniting factor, is a sense that these well-intentioned artists were talking down to the audience. This may explain why even the best-performing of the three artists' releases of the song stalled at 67 on the *Billboard* country singles chart.

The album's first Bob Dylan original: 'Driftin' Too Far From Shore' – the title of which recalls the 1930s gospel song 'Drifting Too Far From the Shore' (recorded by Hank Williams and many others) – is a significant improvement on the last track. While not quite a classic Dylan kiss-off song, it finds him in sufficiently prickly mood with quips like 'I never could guess your weight, baby/Never needed to call you my whore.' The synthesizers and drum sound – both added well after the initial 1984 recording – deprive the song of some potential impact, but Ron Wood's guitar still cuts through that veneer, as do vocals from a studio iteration of the Queens of Rhythm. While not as bitter as some of Dylan's other compositions in this vein, the singer's engagement with the other party makes it feel more personal. His desire to move on calls to mind the dynamics of the *Empire Burlesque* song 'Seeing The Real You At Last.'

Never more do I wonder
Why you don't never play with me anymore
At any moment you could go under
'Cause you're drifting too far from shore

Even by the fragmented measure of this particular album, Dylan's arrangement of the traditional hymn 'Precious Memories' hits a discordant note. Sandwiched between a pair of new compositions displaying jaded views of love, a nostalgic reminiscence of youth feels out of place. With a more understated production, the track might've come across as a modulation of the overall mood, but featuring steel drums as one of the more prominent mix elements, it simply feels perverse.

'Maybe Someday' – the only other song here composed solely by Dylan – covers similar ground as 'Driftin' Too Far From Shore', but from a slightly different perspective. Where that song suggests a dialogue with its subject (target?), 'Maybe Someday' plays more like a monologue: a fairly verbose one of very recent vintage. Though the basic track was another loose thread from the *Empire Burlesque* sessions, the lyrics weren't added until May 1986. In keeping with the overall album, the words reflect a mixed bag of fixations:

> Maybe someday you'll hear a voice from on high
> Sayin', 'For whose sake did you live, for whose sake did you die?'
> Forgive me, baby, for what I didn't do
> For not breakin' down no bedroom door to get at you

Another piece that started life during the recording of *Empire Burlesque* was *Knocked Out Loaded*'s most acclaimed song, 'Brownsville Girl', which started (and dominated) the record's second side. Its multiple layers of inspiration make it one of Dylan's most metatextual works. In his interview with Bill Flanagan for the book *Written in My Soul*, Dylan described how he and Sam Shepard were inspired to write the song (originally known as 'New Danville Girl') after hearing Lou Reed's 'Doin' The Things That We Want To' – the first verse of which talked about seeing Shepard's play *Fool for Love*. According to Dylan, the decision to open 'Brownsville Girl' with the narrator describing a movie, consciously echoed the description of watching the play in Reed's song. Dylan and Shepard ran with that setup – blurring the lines between movies and the narrative throughout 'Brownsville Girl.'

> Something about that movie though, well I just can't get it out of my head
> But I can't remember why I was in it or what part I was supposed to play
> All I remember about it was Gregory Peck and the way people moved
> And a lot of them seemed to be lookin' my way

Despite its scope, the song's melody is fairly simple, but the use of horns and the contributions of the background singers add considerably to the texture. However, the fundamental element of this gospel-western hybrid is Dylan's laconic vocal. In addition to sustaining the whole narrative, his delivery helps lines like 'If there's an original thought out there, I could use it right now' land perfectly. On an album with relatively few new Dylan songs, lines like that make the temptation to ascribe biographical significance to the lyrics difficult to resist. That said, the lines that seem most likely to be a comment on his critics come near the end when the narrator declares, 'I don't have any regrets/They can talk about me plenty when I'm gone.'

With the ascendancy of compact discs, the concept of album sides became less important over the course of the 1980s. Nevertheless, the expectation remained that artists would start an album – however, it was presented – with the strongest, most engaging material. Dylan did very much the opposite on *Knocked Out Loaded*, putting three of the album's four best tracks on the second side. Coincidentally or not, these were also its most collaborative pieces.

'Got My Mind Made Up' – the record's lone collaboration with Tom Petty and The Heartbreakers – isn't as impressive as 'Brownsville Girl', but is still an enjoyable rocker. While Petty and his band also recorded a version of the song, Dylan devised a new set of lyrics for the *Knocked Out Loaded* recording. Anyone looking for the singer within the song, will find satisfaction here:

Don't ever try to change me
I been in this thing too long
There's nothing you can say or do
To make me think I'm wrong

Even with Dylan singing, 'Got My Mind Made Up' sounds more representative of Tom Petty and The Heartbreakers – particularly the group's next album: 1987's *Let Me Up (I've Had Enough.)* Perhaps the song would've found its identity on stage, but it only made the setlist once, on the first show of the True Confessions Tour's North American leg in June 1986. It was still the closest thing the album had to a hit though, reaching the Top 30 on *Billboard*'s Mainstream Rock chart.

The album's final song – 'Under Your Spell' – stands as one of Bob Dylan's most convoluted collaborations. The song's genesis goes back to his 1985 jam sessions with Dave Stewart. Having developed an instrumental track to his liking, Dylan approached songwriter Carole Bayer Sager. Superficially, a composer whose best-known work includes a Broadway musical and an Oscar-winning hit song, was an unlikely partner, but he was clearly casting a wide net for inspiration at this point. In this instance, though, the degree of inspiration is hard to quantify. Sager told Howard Sounes that working on the song 'was probably one of the least collaborative experiences I had with anybody.' She noted that very few of her lyrical ideas made the song's final version: most notably its title. On Dylan's albums earlier in the decade, this kind of reminiscence for an old lover would typically be fueled by apocalyptic urgency, but on this record, the reverie is more low key.

> I was knocked out and loaded in the naked night
> When my last dream exploded, I noticed your light
> Baby, oh what a story I could tell

After finishing *Knocked Out Loaded*, Dylan continued rehearsals for the summer portion of his tour with Tom Petty and The Heartbreakers. Before the first official show, they played a brief set on the 6 June 1986 date of Amnesty International's Conspiracy of Hope tour – a series of six concerts headlined by U2 and Sting celebrating the 25th anniversary of the organization's founding. While Dylan only appeared at the Los Angeles show, Joan Baez incorporating 'The Times They Are A-Changin'' into her sets – and the use of 'I Shall Be Released' as a finale – ensured Dylan retained a presence throughout the tour.

Three days later, the True Confessions Tour resumed with a performance in San Diego. By this point – just five days after their very private marriage ceremony – Carolyn Dennis was back in the lineup for the Queens of Rhythm. Because her mother Madelyn Quebec remained part of the ensemble, Dylan found himself sharing the stage with both his new wife and his mother-in-law, though that aspect wasn't known to the public until many years later.

The makeup of the shows remained much the same as those in Oceania and Japan – Dylan sang a mix of established favorites, recent songs and covers with the band and solo, and Tom Petty and the Heartbreakers performed two short sets of their own. A portion of their Buffalo, New York show on the 4th of July was transmitted by satellite as part of the second Farm Aid concert. The Buffalo concert was also one of several on the tour where they shared billing with the Grateful Dead – and in a foreshadowing of future events, Dylan joined the Dead for their encore at a show in Washington, D.C.

In August, shortly after the tour's final show, Bob Dylan flew to England to play a role in a largely-forgotten movie called *Hearts of Fire*, which also starred largely-forgotten pop singer Fiona (Flanagan) and Rupert Everett (who's maintained a prolific film career in spite of such missteps.) In conjunction with acting in the film, Dylan recorded a handful of songs for the soundtrack, and BBC journalist Christopher Sykes interviewed him for *Getting to Dylan*: an installment of the arts-oriented documentary *Omnibus*. When referring to Bob Dylan talking about himself, terms like candid and revealing often seem like a stretch, but his responses to Sykes' questions at the very least came across as quite thoughtful.

Around this time, Dylan became acquainted with Brooklyn rapper Kurtis Blow, who asked him to record a brief segment for a song called 'Street Rock.' Dylan arguably got the better end of the deal. Neither the song nor the album containing it was a hit, but Dylan later spoke of his appreciation for Blow introducing him to other rap artists such as Ice-T and Public Enemy. Though his latest recordings suggested uncertainty about the idea of being a contemporary artist, he continued to embrace new music that he saw as telling the truth.

The singer was likewise happy to celebrate one of his favorite musicians. Gordon Lightfoot had also been managed by Albert Grossman early in his career, and Lightfoot's 'Early Morning Rain' was one of the many cover songs Dylan recorded for his polarizing 1970 double-album *Self Portrait*. In November 1986, he appeared at the Juno Awards to mark Gordon Lightfoot's induction into the Canadian Music Hall of Fame.

1987: If There's An Original Thought Out There, I Could Use It Right Now

> My audience or future audience now would never be able to experience the newly-plowed fields that I was about to enter. There were many reasons for this, reasons for the whiskey to have gone out of the bottle. Always prolific but never exact, too many distractions had turned my musical path into a jungle of vines. I'd been following established customs and they weren't working. The windows had been boarded up for years and covered with cobwebs, and it's not like I didn't know it.

Several elements make Bob Dylan's 2004 autobiography *Chronicles: Volume One* a fascinating read, not just in comparison to other rock music memoirs, but in general. In addition to how he uses language, it's also striking for the surprising choices of which parts of his life and work it focuses on, and the apparent candor displayed in recounting the events of those chosen periods. With any figure who's known for evasion, the appearance of candor sometimes invites suspicion, especially since Dylan's specifics on dates and places don't always add up. However, sections such as his harsh account of 1987 – a low point for him in virtually everyone's estimation (including his own) – point to a substantial degree of honesty on his part.

Compared to 1982 – the previous year in which Dylan didn't release a solo album – 1987 was very active. He played concerts on multiple continents, began work on a new album, and also appeared on other artists' records. That said, active and productive are very different things. His efforts may have increased what he once referred to as his 'treasure on Earth', but for the most part, they fell short of significance.

The overriding theme for the year was his struggle with how to be the Bob Dylan that audiences expected. He wasn't alone in this position. Many of rock music's legendary figures – at least those lucky enough to still have record contracts – spent at least a portion of the 1980s struggling commercially and/or artistically. Caught between their revered early work and their status as elder statesmen – neither the leading edge nor institutions – they collectively made a compelling case for there being no stage more difficult for an influential artist than middle age. With both commercial and critical success proving elusive, Dylan experienced the disconnect between the regard for his older work and the reception of his new albums, more than most.

Regardless of how audiences saw him, Dylan was happy to pay tribute to others. On 11 March 11, he appeared at the Gershwin Gala, honoring the music of both George and Ira Gershwin. Held at the Brooklyn Academy of Music, his fellow performers ran the gamut from Leonard Bernstein to Madeline Kahn. Working with guitarist Ted Perlman – who played on *Empire Burlesque* and was married to Peggi Blu from the Queens of Rhythm – Dylan developed an arrangement of the Gershwin's song 'Soon'. His performance stood out for a couple of reasons. Along with 'Soon' being a relatively obscure Gershwin composition – introduced in a 1930 rewrite of the musical *Strike Up the Band* – the approach Dylan took was unconventional by his own standards. As Ted Perlman put it, 'He actually was singing, not doing his Bob voice'. Dylan's abiding interest in the American songbook would adopt a more-concrete form three decades later with a trio of studio albums full of pop standards – including the 2015 Frank Sinatra tribute *Shadows in the Night*.

Also in March 1987, U2 released their fifth studio album *The Joshua Tree*. In the three years since Bono interviewed Dylan before his performance at Slane Castle, the Irish band's following had expanded immensely. *The Joshua Tree* was an instant hit, completing the rise to worldwide stardom that their breakout performance at Live Aid had already accelerated. While not renowned for their humility, U2 happily acknowledged their musical precursors. Their Live Aid performance incorporated songs by The Rolling Stones and Lou Reed, and 'Knockin' on Heaven's Door' was a regular part of the encore on the 1985 Unforgettable Fire Tour. At an April-1987 concert in Los Angeles, Dylan joined the band for that song as well as 'I Shall Be Released.'

As the band toured the US for *The Joshua Tree*, they were also looking ahead to their next musical project: the album and movie *Rattle and Hum*. The movie turned out to be a fairly standard rock-tour documentary – a bit more pretentious than some, though bolstered by strong live performances – but the accompanying album was more successful. A mix of live and studio recordings, the *Rattle and Hum* album also paid tribute to U2's musical idols throughout: particularly Bob Dylan. In addition to the group's live performance of 'All Along the Watchtower,' the album featured two songs Dylan also performed on – 'Hawkmoon 269' and 'Love Rescue Me,' the latter of which he co-wrote with the band.

Other artists Dylan recorded with early in the year included Warren Zevon and Ringo Starr, though behind-the-scenes circumstances have kept the recording with the former Beatle from being officially released.

Around this time, Dylan began working on his next record. Like his two previous albums, the overriding approach was periodic recording sessions with a rotating cast of musicians. One of the better-known contributors was guitarist Dave Alvin of the Los Angeles band The Blasters, with whom Dylan apparently discussed plans to make a follow up to *Self Portrait*: his 1970 album spotlighting other artists' songs.

Based on the description Alvin gave Clinton Heylin – of a dynamic session focused on classic country and blues songs, effortlessly changing gears from 'Elvis Sun to Elvis RCA' – it's unfortunate that none of the material has been released. The guitarist recalled that Dylan's apology to him for not using any of these recordings, was followed by the remark, 'You know it's gonna come out one of these days, on one of those box sets!' To date, this hasn't happened, which seems fitting for an album delayed from release until the following year due to second thoughts on song selection.

In May, Dylan resolved one long-running matter while setting forth on a short-term collaboration, both of which had significant financial implications. The protracted legal fight with Albert Grossman over royalties for Dylan's early work was nearing the five-year mark when Grossman died on a flight to London in January 1986. His delaying tactics – some of them rather questionable – outlasted Grossman himself, but his widow Sally continued the legal fight for over a year until Dylan finally agreed to settle the case. In the short term, the deal cost him about $3,000,000, but set the stage for him to gain control of the rights to all of his music publishing (the endgame of which was the $300,000,000 sale of his song catalog to Universal Music Publishing in 2020).

This large legal bill, along with friendship with Jerry Garcia, enticed Dylan to agree to a brief summer tour with the Grateful Dead. Along with being fans of Dylan's music, the Dead had remained a major concert draw in the US despite them going several years between albums, and their forthcoming album would be one of the most successful of their long career. On paper, it was an extremely favorable arrangement for Dylan – performing one set during each show, but still receiving the majority of proceeds the huge audiences brought in.

But there was a paradoxical downside. Unlike the previous year's tour with Tom Petty and The Heartbreakers – which revolved around a fairly consistent selection of songs – the Dead envisioned a more expansive setlist. But at this point, Dylan believed that the vast majority of his songs were beyond his capacity to perform, and that he 'was no longer capable of doing anything radically creative with them.' This combined with a recognition that the crowds at his concerts owed more to the bands he was playing with than his own stature, during rehearsals, he considered backing out of the tour.

Though Dylan's desire to rehearse any given song only a couple of times before moving on to something else frustrated some members of the Grateful Dead, both parties persevered. Their six shows together may not have been a high point for either entity but were worthwhile on their own terms. *Dylan & the Dead* – the live album released in 1989 – shows the tour to have been a very uneven affair, but any circumstance that involved the first-ever live performances of 'Queen Jane Approximately', added at least something of value to Dylan's legacy.

Dylan & the Dead (1989)

Personnel:
Bob Dylan: guitar, vocals
Jerry Garcia: guitar, vocals
Mickey Hart: drums
Bill Kreutzmann: drums
Phil Lesh: bass
Brett Mydland: keyboards, vocals
Bob Weir: guitar, vocals
Producers: Jerry Garcia, John Cutler
Engineers: John Cutler, Guy Charbonneau, Gary Hedden, David Roberts, Peter Miller, Billy Rothschild and Chris Wiskes
Release date: 6 February 1989
Chart places: US: 37, UK: 38
Running time: 43:07
All songs written by Bob Dylan, except 'Joey' by Bob Dylan and Jacques Levy.

Side One: 1. 'Slow Train' 2. 'I Want You' 3. 'Gotta Serve Somebody' 4. 'Queen Jane Approximately'
Side Two: 1. 'Joey' 2. 'All Along The Watchtower' 3. 'Knockin' on Heaven's Door'

The most interesting thing related to Bob Dylan in 1987 is something he might not actually have been involved in. On the eve of the tour with The

Grateful Dead, the 1 July issue of *Esquire* featured a piece by Sam Shepard called 'True Dylan' (later retitled 'A Short Life Of Trouble'). Described as 'A one-act play, as it really happened one afternoon in California,' it's presented as Sam trying to interview a somewhat distracted Bob on topics like Ricky Nelson, Woody Guthrie and, of course, women. 'True Dylan' is a compelling read; the deliberate blurring of fact and fiction offering more questions than answers – Was the depicted conversation derived from one that actually took place, or was it simply Shepard's take on the singer? Was Dylan in on the joke or even aware of it?

Several weeks after his last show with the Dead, Dylan reunited with Tom Petty and The Heartbreakers to perform in the Middle East and Europe: regions not visited on the True Confessions Tour. Billed as the Temples in Flames Tour, this series of concerts found the singer consciously working to vary the setlists. Though he'd later describe this period to journalist Robert Hilburn as a time where 'I didn't feel I knew who I was on stage,' other accounts identify this tour as the point where he had to choose between an artistic dead-end and reconnecting with his sources of inspiration.

In a 1997 *Newsweek* profile – and also in *Chronicles: Volume One* – Dylan talked about an October show in Locarno, Switzerland, where the techniques he'd been using to get through shows failed him. Standing on stage at an outdoor venue with thousands of fans watching, a thought came to him – 'I'm determined to stand whether God will deliver me or not' – and he found himself 'a new performer, an unknown one in the true sense of the word.' Fittingly, this show marked the last time to date that he's performed the song 'Trust Yourself' in concert.

The tour with Tom Petty wrapped up in mid-October with four shows at London's Wembley Arena. The following month, the British theatrical release of *Hearts of Fire* provided another public embodiment of a disappointing year. Relatively few people are qualified to assess whether casting Dylan in the role of reclusive rock star Billy Parker was brilliant or a bit too obvious. The movie performed poorly in the UK, and bypassed theaters for a direct-to-video release in the US a couple of years later. As for the movie's out-of-print soundtrack, it invites curiosity – not so much for Dylan's three contributions or the five songs sung by Fiona, but rather for Rupert Everett's take on Soft Cell's hit 'Tainted Love'. In fairness to Dylan, the soundtrack omits his engaging (and engaged) performance of Shel Silverstein's 'A Couple More Years': a song he'd included in his setlist for multiple shows in 1980. However, even with Fiona's pop-metal title track setting the bar low, this left Dylan's rendition of John Hiatt's 'The Usual' as the album's only real standout. The airplay it received on US album-rock stations when released as a single, makes it the most successful thing about *Hearts of Fire*.

By the end of the year, Dylan had begun a wholesale rethink of his working methods, and set plans in motion for a tour he believed would enable him to reconnect with his songs. However, before the results could reach fruition, he had to work through a few more challenges.

1988: Stake My Future on a Hell of a Past

Bruce Springsteen's remarks given when inducting Bob Dylan into the Rock and Roll Hall of Fame on 20 January 1988, could not have been more complimentary:

> He had the vision and the talent to make a pop song that contained the whole world. He invented a new way a pop singer could sound, broke through the limitations of what a recording artist could achieve, and changed the face of rock and roll forever.

Under other circumstances, these remarks could easily have been ingredients in the recipe for another year of artistic drift. An upcoming album embodying Dylan's creative uncertainty, and plaudits from arguably the most successful *new Dylan* that had emerged in his wake – even if that individual praised Dylan's more recent work – both pointed to an artist existing in the past tense. Dylan however, had something different in mind.

Though *Down in the Groove* wasn't released until a few months later, the inevitable all-star performance of 'All Along The Watchtower' during the Hall of Fame induction ceremony, arguably marked the *real* end-point for Dylan's protracted period of uncertainty. With far too many performers on the stage, the song felt languid rather than urgent, and his friend (and fellow inductee) George Harrison seemingly had to talk Dylan into singing it. A more satisfying collaboration with Harrison would soon take shape, but for the most part, the induction ceremony was the kind of environment Dylan was looking to escape from.

Another factor that doubtless contributed to Dylan being tentative, was an arm injury that occurred on the grounds of his Malibu home late the previous year. In *Chronicles*, he recounted his worries that the damage to his hand meant the end of his days playing guitar. Fortunately, those fears were misplaced, allowing for a year that was both active and consequential.

Conventional wisdom excludes the album *Down in the Groove* – released in May after a delay of several months – from the equation of Dylan's artistic renaissance. While this is understandable, it's also somewhat reductive. *Down in the Groove* is a far more interesting record than is generally acknowledged, if only as a point of comparison with the work that followed. Between the struggle to write new songs, seemingly random assemblages of musicians, and an ill-advised trip to the outtakes well, the album encapsulates his musical identity crisis in this period. On the plus side, Dylan being hard-pressed to come up with new compositions, resulted in some excellent renditions of songs by others. But based on *Down in the Groove*'s poor sales and bad reviews, that wasn't what fans or critics wanted to hear. In fairness to Dylan, both of those groups would've been hard-pressed to articulate what they *did* want to hear from him without referring to past successes. For the singer's part, he had largely moved beyond worrying about it by this point.

Down in the Groove (1988)

Personnel:

1.'Let's Stick Together' (Wilbert Harrison)
Bob Dylan – vocals, guitar and harmonica: Danny Kortchmar – guitar: Steve Jordan – drums: Randy Jackson – bass

2.'When Did You Leave Heaven?' (Walter Bullock, Richard Whiting)
Bob Dylan – vocals, guitar: Madelyn Quebec – vocals, keyboards: Stephen Shelton – drums

3.'Sally Sue Brown' (Arthur June Alexander, Earl Montgomery, Tom Stanford)
Bob Dylan – vocals, guitar: Steve Jones – guitar: Myron Grambacher – drums: Paul Simonon – bass: Kevin Savigar – keyboards: Madelyn Quebec – vocals: Bobby King and Willie Green – background vocals

4.'Death Is Not The End'
Bob Dylan – vocals, guitar and harmonica: Clydie King – background vocals: Mark Knopfler – guitar: Robbie Shakespeare – bass: Sly Dunbar – drums: Alan Clark – keyboards: Full Force – background vocals

5.'Had A Dream About You, Baby'
Bob Dylan – vocals, guitar: Eric Clapton – guitar: Ron Wood – bass: Kip Winger – bass: Beau Hill – keyboards: Mitchell Froom – keyboards: Henry Spinetti – drums

6.'Ugliest Girl In The World' (Bob Dylan, Robert Hunter)
Bob Dylan – vocals, guitar: Danny Kortchmar – guitar: Steve Jordan – drums: Randy Jackson – bass: Stephen Shelton – keyboards: Madelyn Quebec and Carolyn Dennis – background vocals

7.'Silvio' (Bob Dylan, Robert Hunter)
Bob Dylan – vocals, guitar: Nathan East – bass: Mike Baird – drums: Madelyn
Quebec and Carolyn Dennis – background vocals: Jerry Garcia, Bob Weir and
Brett Mydland – additional vocals

8.'Ninety Miles An Hour (Down A Dead End Street)' (Hal Blair, Don Robertson)
Bob Dylan – vocals, guitar: Madelyn Quebec – vocals, keyboards: Willie Green
and Bobby King – background vocals

9.'Shenandoah' (Trad. arr Bob Dylan)
Bob Dylan – vocals, guitar and harmonica: Nathan East – bass: Madelyn
Quebec, Carolyn Dennis, Peggi Blu and Alexandra Brown – background vocals

10.'Rank Strangers To Me' (Albert E. Brumley)
Bob Dylan – vocals, guitar: Larry Klein – bass

Producer: Uncredited, except 'Death Is Not The End' produced by Bob Dylan and
Mark Knopfler
Engineers: Stephen Shelton, Cake Johnson ('Sally Sue Brown'), Mike Kloster, Brian
Soucy, Jeff Musel and Jeff Preziosi
Mixing: Stephen Shelton
Release date: US: 31 May 1988, UK: June 1988
Chart places: US: 61, UK: 32
Running Time: 32:10
Songs by Bob Dylan except as noted

Down in the Groove echoes *Knocked Out Loaded*'s move of opening with
a cover song. 'Kansas City' singer Wilbert Harrison's 'Let's Stick Together'
is best-known from Bryan Ferry's 1976 recording. Harrison's original
recording didn't chart, but Ferry's version was a hit twice, reaching
number 4 in the UK on its original release, and hitting 12 when reissued
in a remixed form in 1988. Dylan's straightforward rendition displays
his obvious affection for this portrayal of love at the crossroads, even if it
doesn't necessarily add much to it.

From an R&B classic, the album moves to the pop standard 'When
Did You Leave Heaven?' Recorded by a wide range of artists across a
variety of styles, the song demonstrates the breadth of Dylan's musical
influences. Aside from drummer Stephen Shelton, the only other musician
accompanying Dylan is Madelyn Quebec, who sings and plays keyboards.

Though Dylan was newly married to Carolyn Dennis when *Down in the Groove* was recorded, he seemed more interested in recording with his mother-in-law. Quebec appears on six of the album's ten songs, while her daughter can only be heard on three.

'Sally Sue Brown' was soul singer Arthur Alexander's first single. Dylan wasn't the only artist of his generation to cover Alexander's songs, but The Rolling Stones and The Hollies did so much earlier in their careers. As latter-day tributes go, however, Dylan was slightly ahead of the curve. After Alexander passed away in 1993, the tribute album *Adios Amigo* brought together interpretations of his work by performers ranging from Roger McGuinn and Living Colour singer Corey Glover, to Elvis Costello, who contributed his own rendition of 'Sally Sue Brown.'

In keeping with the grab-bag approach of *Down in the Groove*, its first Dylan composition is an outtake from *Infidels*. 'Death Is Not The End' was among the last things recorded during sessions for that album in 1983. Lyrics about cities 'on fire with the burning flesh of men' align the song with its apocalyptic brethren, but the languid presentation ensures that the persistent questions about leaving songs like 'Blind Willie McTell' off of *Infidels* would not be repeated in this instance. Arguably, the most noteworthy aspect of 'Death Is Not The End' is that – unlike his previous repurposed recording from that album: 'Tight Connection To My Heart' – Dylan retained Knopfler's instrumental contribution.

While the track that closes the first side is not prime Bob Dylan, for better or worse, it's at least a relatively fresh example of his craft. 'Had A Dream About You, Baby' was initially recorded for the soundtrack to *Hearts of Fire*. Lyrically, the song reflects Dylan at his most ordinary:

You got the crazy rhythm when you walk
You make me nervous when you start to talk

The recording is noteworthy mainly for the musicians accompanying Dylan, especially Eric Clapton and Ron Wood. If the decision to include this song on *Down in the Groove* rather than *Hearts of Fire*'s genuine highlight 'The Usual' suggests affection trumping artistic judgment, the affection was short-lived. Dylan played 'Had A Dream About You, Baby' a few times on tour that year, but it's otherwise been forgotten.

On balance, *Down in the Groove*'s second side is stronger, but also opens with one of Dylan's more puzzling songs. One of two lyrical collaborations with Robert Hunter – best known for writing songs with

the Grateful Dead – 'The Ugliest Girl In The World' was presumably
intended as a joke. Whatever the intentions, nothing about the song or
Dylan's performance was likely to change the mind of listeners put off by
lyric lapses like 'a woman like you should be at home' from 'Sweetheart
Like You'. Perhaps Carolyn Dennis and Madelyn Quebec's interjections of
'She's so ugly' are meant as a humorous counterpoint, but their delivery
is along the same lines as their other performances with the Queens of
Rhythm.

The other Robert Hunter collaboration – 'Silvio' – turned out much
better. With the Grateful Dead still riding high from their comeback album
In the Dark, the presence of Jerry Garcia, Bob Weir and Brett Mydland
made the song an obvious focal point for promoting the album. Though
this didn't translate to sales, the song got significant airplay on album-rock
stations and reached number 5 on *Billboard*'s mainstream rock chart,
thanks to an agreeable groove and pleasantly thoughtful lyrics.

> I will sing it loud and sing it strong
> Let the echo decide if I was right or wrong

If more of the performances from the 1987 tour with the Grateful Dead
had displayed the energy 'Silvio' does, that tour would probably have
a much better reputation. As it stands, the only songs Dylan performed
more often in 1988 were 'Like A Rolling Stone' and 'Subterranean
Homesick Blues.' In contrast, the far-more-acclaimed 'Every Grain of
Sand' was played just a handful of times that year, and historically has
been featured in concert a fraction as often.

Down in the Groove closes with three interpretations of songs by
others. Bearing in mind Dylan's tumultuous personal life – even during
his marriage to Carolyn Dennis – he could probably relate to the classic
country song 'Ninety Miles An Hour (Down A Dead End Street)' better
than most. The combination of religious and racing imagery, lends this
tale of illicit romance an appropriately dramatic atmosphere.

> As a bad motorcycle with the devil in the seat
> Going ninety miles an hour down a dead end street

Along with 'Silvio', Dylan's lovely arrangement of the 19th-century
American folk song 'Shenandoah' is the highlight of the album. Despite
having just one additional instrumentalist – bassist Nathan East – the

recording is exceedingly dynamic, thanks to the vocal contributions of the Queens of Rhythm. *Down in the Groove* was his last album to feature the female background singers that had been so much a part of his sound for a decade. Dylan enjoyed trying out vocal arrangements while on tour with them. Most of these went unheard, but this particular track might be their single best performance.

The album closes with the gospel music standard 'Rank Strangers To Me.' Written in 1942 by the remarkably prolific Albert E. Brumley, and popularized through The Stanley Brothers' 1960 recording, the song became a quintessential example of *stained glass bluegrass*. Other bluegrass artists to record the song include Ricky Skaggs and Doc Watson, while renditions from Pat Boone and country legend Porter Wagoner demonstrate its broader reach. Though the song is informed by reckoning with one's mortality, it ends the album on a hopeful note:

> They all moved away, said the voice of a stranger
> To that beautiful shore by the bright crystal sea
> Some beautiful day I'll meet 'em in heaven
> Where no one will be a stranger to me

The song's message found an earthly match in Dylan's new approach as both a writer and performer. The lengthy interval between recording *Down in the Groove* and the album's release, obscured the process, but it was well underway by the time 'Silvio' started playing on US radio stations. It began during the previous year's tours with the Grateful Dead and Tom Petty and The Heartbreakers, when Dylan recognized the need to engage with his songs beyond the relative handful he felt comfortable with. After these tours – where the majority of fans were coming to see the bands he was performing with – he also felt a need to engage with the audience on a different level.

Whether alive or dead, most of rock music's icons have a dual existence, with the full range of their work only known to a minority of fans and overshadowed by the inevitable greatest-hits/classic-rock incarnation. The latter is typically defined by a dozen or so songs consistently played in concert, collected on compilations and/or heard via the contemporary equivalents of album-rock radio stations. A few of these tracks might hint at the artist's other existence, but overall, the broader scope of their work is left underappreciated: frequently by the artists themselves as much as the audiences. This was the position Dylan found himself in during his mid-1980s tours, and he decided that the path forward required more than simply expanding his setlist. Reflecting on this time in *Chronicles*, he recognized the role audience expectations played, especially in an arena or stadium setting:

> I definitely needed a new audience, because my audience at that time had more or less grown up on my records and was past the point of accepting me as a new artist, and this was understandable. In many ways, this audience was past its prime, and its reflexes were shot. They came to stare and not participate. That was okay, but the kind of crowd that would have to find me, would be the kind of crowd that didn't know what yesterday was.

One of the few analogues to the scope of this rethink of the relationship between an artist and their audience, was Dylan's initial 1979-1980 Gospel Tour. Along similar lines to that tour, he now decided to forego larger venues in favor of smaller theaters, and committed himself to a consistent schedule of shows in this vein that came to be known as the Never Ending Tour: another common label the singer has largely disavowed. From 1988 through to 2019, Dylan played 70 or more shows a year, stopping only as the COVID-19 pandemic emerged.

The other part of the equation was songwriting. After a few years of writing very little – and being more dependent than usual on collaborators for what he did write – the singer had a flurry of songs come to him early in 1988. Despite some initial hesitancy about whether he actually wanted to record these new compositions, a different opportunity to display his renewed creativity emerged somewhat out of the blue.

George Harrison was among the few rock artists of his generation, enjoying both critical and commercial success in the spring of 1988. His first album in five years – *Cloud Nine* – received favorable comparisons to his landmark album *All Things Must Pass*, and reached the Top 10 in both the US and the UK. Called upon to record a B-side for an upcoming single, Harrison enlisted his *Cloud Nine* co-producer – the Electric Light Orchestra's Jeff Lynne – who was working on records by Roy Orbison and Tom Petty at the time. After Dylan agreed to let them use his home studio, Petty and Orbison joined Harrison and Lynne there, and with help from drummer Jim Keltner, the quintet wrote and recorded the song 'Handle With Care' in a single day. Executives at Warner Bros. – which distributed

Harrison's records at the time – determined that 'Handle With Care' was too good for such a limited use, leaving the former Beatle wondering what to do with it. Having captured lightning in a bottle once, he decided to try nine more times, and the *de facto* band reconvened in May – this time at Dave Stewart's house – to write and record a full album. The timing – which was dictated by the tour Dylan was scheduled to begin in June – necessitated writing a new song each day.

The need to work quickly worked in the album's favor. Even Jeff Lynne – famous for being fastidious in the studio – agreed. He told an interviewer for a 1989 *Rolling Stone* piece: 'That's why the songs are so good and fresh – because they hadn't been second-guessed and dissected and replaced.' This loose approach carried through to the group's public presentation.

While many supergroups are better remembered for the fame and/or egos of those involved than their music, The Traveling Wilburys attained the opposite result. Purposely downplaying the status of the members, they adopted the finest rock music alter-egos since Ziggy Stardust – a quintet of half-brothers, all of them sons of the somewhat disreputable Charles Truscott Wilbury. This kept attention more focused on the songs, while sidestepping the outsized expectations the individual participants would otherwise generate.

The band's fictional history was detailed in the liner notes by Hugh Jampton of the University of Krakatoa. According to Mr. Jampton – better-known as Monty Python's Michael Palin, who had appeared in multiple films from Harrison's production company Handmade Films (most prominently *Monty Python's Life of Brian*):

> The original Wilburys were a stationary people who – realising that their civilisation could not stand still forever – began to go for short walks.

In this telling, the album's songs 'represent the popular laments; the epic and heroic tales which characterise the apotheosis of the elusive Wilbury sound.'

In real-world terms, the name had its origins in a joke between Harrison and Lynne. When they ran into technical glitches during the recording of *Cloud Nine*, Harrison joked, 'We'll bury 'em in the mix.' The term endured as a private joke before finding its more public expression. Harrison initially suggested The Trembling Wilburys as the group name, which Lynne suggested changing to The Traveling Wilburys.

When released in October 1988, critical and commercial reception were both very favorable. *Rolling Stone* reviewer David Wild called the record 'a low-key masterpiece,' and it quickly reached the Top 10 in numerous countries, including the United States where it sold 3,000,000 copies. More importantly, the group created an album that felt warmhearted, fun and effortless. That's not to say it wasn't well-crafted – no album with Jeff Lynne as producer could be otherwise – but rather that it didn't feel labored.

The Traveling Wilburys Vol. 1 (1988)
Personnel:
Otis Wilbury (Jeff Lynne): keyboards, guitars, vocals
Nelson Wilbury (George Harrison): guitars, vocals
Charlie T Junior (Tom Petty): acoustic guitar, vocals
Lefty Wilbury (Roy Orbison): acoustic guitar, vocals
Lucky Wilbury (Bob Dylan): acoustic guitar, vocals
Jim Keltner: drums
Jim Horn: saxophone
Ray Cooper: percussion
Ian Wallace: tom toms ('Handle With Care')
Producers: Otis and Nelson Wilbury
Engineers: Richard Dodd, Phil MacDonald, Don Smith and Bill Bottrell
Release date: US: 18 October 1988, UK: 24 October 1988
Chart places: US: 3, UK: 16
Running Time: 36:20
All songs jointly written by The Traveling Wilburys, with primary writers noted below.

Side One: 1. 'Handle With Care' (Harrison) 2. 'Dirty World' (Dylan) 3. 'Rattled' (Lynne) 4. 'Last Night' (Petty) 5. 'Not Alone Anymore' (Lynne)
Side Two: 1. 'Congratulations' (Dylan) 2. 'Heading for the Light' (Harrison) 3. 'Margarita' (Petty) 4. 'Tweeter and the Monkey Man' (Dylan) 5. 'End of the Line' (Harrison)

While some members' contributions were more apparent vocally, the overriding sense was still that of a larger group working in tandem to bring each other's strengths to the forefront. This applies to the songwriting as well. All of the songs on *The Traveling Wilburys Vol. 1* were credited to the group as a whole on the initial release, and according to Lynne, each of them reflects contributions from the various members.

Nevertheless, it was fairly clear which songs had Dylan (aka Lucky Wilbury) as their primary writer, just as it was clear that these three songs were some of his best work in years.

Dylan led with his sense of humor on the first of his contributions: 'Dirty World.' Though the end result is quite different musically from its supposed origins as an attempt to do a song like Prince, it outpaces 'Little Red Corvette' in its deployment of automotive metaphor. Printed lyrics don't do the song justice, because Dylan's perfectly executed phrasing is so instrumental to the joke:

> You don't need no wax job
> You're smooth enough for me
> If you need your oil changed
> I'll do it for you free
> Oh baby, the pleasure would be all mine
> If you let me drive your pickup truck
> And park it where the sun don't shine

'Congratulations' – which opens side two – is more downbeat but no less in keeping with the album's emphasis on middle-age concerns. Another example of a Dylan ode to love gone wrong, its balance of curt phrasing and wistfulness, distinguishes it. Lines like 'Congratulations, how good you must feel' are counterpointed by the more reflective verse lyrics:

> And if I had just one more chance to win your heart again
> I would do things differently
> But what's the use to pretend?

The most memorable and ambitious song of the three, truly shows Dylan's return to form. 'Tweeter And The Monkey Man' was immediately pegged as a takeoff on the musical and (especially) verbal sprawl of Bruce Springsteen's early work. A reference to his song 'Thunder Road' and the lyric 'In Jersey anything's legal, as long as you don't get caught', certainly support that hypothesis. However, as much as the New Jersey setting evokes Springsteen, it also calls to mind one of Dylan's most famous songs. Not only did 'the story of the Hurricane' unfold in the same state, its protagonist Rubin Carter was wrongfully imprisoned in Rahway State Prison (since renamed): a location specifically referenced in the Wilburys song. In addition to echoing the approach of 'Hurricane' and Dylan's other narrative-driven songs – where the words provide as much momentum as the music – 'Tweeter and the Monkey Man' provides a useful point of comparison with some of Dylan's recent prior efforts in this vein. As good as songs such as 'When the Night Comes Falling From the Sky' are, they sometimes sound like they're straining to achieve significance. 'Tweeter and the Monkey Man' – which Dylan recorded in two takes – comes across as being unconcerned with such things, establishing a complicated narrative with great lyric economy, and happy to be taken on its own terms.

> Tweeter and the Monkey Man were hard up for cash
> They stayed up all night selling cocaine and hash
> To an undercover cop who had a sister named Jan
> For reasons unexplained, she loved the Monkey Man

Though all of the Wilburys reaped the benefit of their collaboration, Dylan arguably gained the most. Whether it was a function of his illustrious peers challenging him artistically or simply providing a comfortable setting for making music, the time spent as Lucky Wilbury seemed to help him remember how to be Bob Dylan again.

Above all, The Traveling Wilburys album achieved George Harrison's primary goal of the project, not compromising their friendships. Though Roy Orbison's death in December 1988 prevented the full lineup from recording again, the remaining members all played music with each other again in some combination, including another Wilburys album, released in 1990. *Traveling Wilburys Vol. 3* – as the second album was dubbed – was less successful than the first, but the Wilburys sound – classic rock and roll with just the right amount of high-tech sheen – remained a significant part of the pop music landscape for the next couple years. Both Tom Petty's solo album *Full Moon Fever* and Roy Orbison's posthumous release *Mystery Girl* – each of which featured production by Lynne – were major hits.

Among the group, Bob Dylan was alone in not exploring this approach further on his own albums. Despite him writing an album's worth of new songs, he wasn't certain he wanted to record a new solo album. Bono suggested that Dylan talk to Daniel Lanois – who had produced U2's last two album's with Brian Eno – as someone whose musical ideas would mesh with Dylan's own.

In the short term, Dylan remained focused on live performances. On 7 June, he opened his new tour in Concord, California, with a guest appearance from Neil Young, but otherwise accompanied by the smallest band Dylan had fronted in a long time. The trio included bassist Kenny Aaronson, drummer Christopher Parker and guitarist G. E. Smith – best known for his tenure as Hall & Oates' lead guitarist, and a decade-long run as the leader of the *Saturday Night Live* house band. The setlist – which included songs from 1963's *The Freewheelin' Bob Dylan* to *Knocked Out Loaded* – along with some well-chosen covers – set the template for the hundreds of shows to follow over the next couple of decades.

When the tour came to New Orleans in September, Dylan and Lanois discussed the possibility of working on an album together. At the time, Lanois was finishing up production of *Yellow Moon* – a new album by The Neville Brothers that coincidentally included their renditions of two older Dylan songs: 'The Ballad pf Hollis Brown' and 'With God On Our Side.' That album would be released in March 1989, shortly after Dylan and Lanois started recording Dylan's final album of the decade.

1989: Stay Right With It When the Road Unwinds

The list of records released in 1989 contains the expected mix of hits from major stars, unfairly overlooked albums by both new and established artists, and the obligatory footnotes to pop music history. Along that continuum, it was an interesting year for some of rock's most storied artists, who – generally speaking – closed out the decade with some of their strongest work in years. The Rolling Stones' *Steel Wheels* aside, these albums weren't big hits. But Paul McCartney's *Flowers in the Dirt*, Lou Reed's *New York* and Neil Young's *Freedom,* all represented returns to form for their respective artists.

Bob Dylan's album *Oh Mercy* is generally grouped with those examples of iconic artists reclaiming relevance in middle age. However, categorizing them this way significantly oversimplifies each of their stories – especially Dylan's. Because the standard Dylan narrative histories often treat The Traveling Wilburys as a detour rather than a meaningful step, *Oh Mercy* can seem like something out of the blue, rather than empirical evidence of a renewed sense of purpose.

The February release of the *Dylan & the Dead* live album understandably reinforced this impression of an artist still somewhat adrift. Reaching the Top 40 on the US album charts, and achieving eventual Gold-record certification, made the album more commercially successful than its immediate predecessors in the Dylan catalog, but the music on it still reflected the tentative approach of the singer himself. While the Grateful Dead deserve credit for pushing Dylan to expand his concert repertoire, they didn't always inspire memorable performances of those songs.

Fresh evidence of this phenomenon emerged when the singer joined the Dead on stage in Los Angeles shortly after the live album's release. Guitarist Bob Weir later told Howard Sounes in *Down the Highway: The Life of Bob Dylan*, that shortly after this show, Dylan approached the band about joining them on a regular basis. According to Weir's account, the group seriously considered it, but declined because another band member opposed the move. Based on the available recording of the show, this was a better outcome for all involved.

After several songs where Dylan mainly played guitar – the primary exception being shared vocals on a shambolic rendition of 'Stuck Inside Of Mobile With The Memphis Blues Again' – he returned for the encore, which included 'Knockin' on Heaven's Door.' In contrast to the strong performances of the song on his own tour the previous year, this rendition mirrored the one on *Dylan & the Dead* where the two entities sometimes seemed to be performing different songs.

Dylan's own shows would be on a more solid footing when he resumed touring in May; but before that came the trip to New Orleans to record his new album. Accompanied by Carolyn Dennis (though their marriage remained a closely-held secret), he rented a house there and settled in for several weeks of work with Daniel Lanois.

Renting houses was also part of Lanois's method of record production. Rather than using traditional studios, he would set up recording equipment in older homes. For *Oh Mercy*, this involved multiple houses. With the help of musicians recruited by the producer, Dylan attempted several of his new songs in the historic Emlah Court building – however, the initial results proved frustrating. The location likely had little to do with this, but the musicians soon resumed work in a different building.

While friction between the singer and his latest-chosen producer might superficially seem reminiscent of the *Infidels* sessions, the circumstances were quite different. Where the issues with Mark Knopfler on *Infidels* manifested near the end of the process, the disconnect on *Oh Mercy* took place earlier in the recording, allowing time for Dylan and Lanois to work through it. 'There came this point when Dan finally really lost it with him,' engineer Mark Howard told *Uncut*. 'We walked out and let them sort it out. And then, when we got back, from then on, Dylan was just really pleasant to work with.'

The nature of the two album projects' disagreements *also* differed. Knopfler and Dylan ended up at odds about working methods and musical approach. The problems Dylan and Lanois had seemed rooted in their differing expectations about what they wanted to achieve on the album:

> I wasn't looking to express myself in any kind of new way. All my ways were intact and had been for years. There wasn't much chance in changing now. I didn't need to climb the next mountain. If anything, what I wanted to do was to secure the place where I was at. I wasn't sure Lanois understood that. I guess I never made it plain, couldn't put it in so many words.

Considering the acclaim *Oh Mercy* received upon its release, Dylan's summation of his own goals comes across as surprisingly modest in *Chronicles*. For many years, the benchmark for a good Bob Dylan album was *His-best-since-Blood-on-the-Tracks*. Of his 1980s albums, the label was applied more commonly to *Infidels*, but the designation seems more appropriate to *Oh Mercy*.

Jakob Dylan famously remarked to *Rolling Stone* that listening to *Blood on the Tracks* was like hearing 'my parents talking'. *Oh Mercy* often feels like a conversation between Bob Dylan and himself. A 2019 retrospective piece on the album, aptly described it as sounding 'at once like a sermon, a diary and a faded old photograph': a quality that makes it a fitting bookend for the decade, along with *Saved*.

Oh Mercy (1989)
Personnel:

1.'Political World'
Bob Dylan – vocal, guitar: Daniel Lanois – dobro: Mason Ruffner – guitar: Brian Stoltz – guitar: Tony Hall – bass: Cyril Neville – percussion: Willie Green – drums

2.'Where Teardrops Fall'
Bob Dylan – vocal, piano: Daniel Lanois – lap steel: Paul Synegal – guitar: Larry Jolivet – bass: Alton Rubin Jr. – scrub board: John Hart – saxophone: Rockin' Dopsie – accordion

3.'Everything Is Broken'
Bob Dylan – vocals, guitar and harmonica: Daniel Lanois – dobro: Malcolm Burn – tambourine: Tony Hall – bass: Willie Green – drums: Brian Stoltz – guitar: Daryl Johnson – percussion

4.'Ring Them Bells'
Bob Dylan – vocals, piano: Daniel Lanois – guitar: Malcolm Burn – keyboards

5.'Man In The Long Black Coat'
Bob Dylan – vocal, 6 and 12-string guitars, harmonica: Daniel Lanois – dobro: Malcolm Burn – keyboards

6.'Most Of The Time'
Bob Dylan – vocal, guitar: Daniel Lanois – guitar: Malcolm Burn – keyboards: Tony Hall – bass: Cyril Neville – percussion

7.'What Good Am I?'
Bob Dylan – vocal, guitar and piano: Daniel Lanois – dobro: Malcolm Burn – keys

8.'Disease Of Conceit'
Bob Dylan – vocal, piano and organ: Mason Ruffner – guitar: Brian Stoltz – guitar:
Tony Hall – bass: Willie Green – drums

9.'What Was It You Wanted'
Bob Dylan – vocal, guitar and harmonica: Daniel Lanois – guitar: Malcolm Burn –
bass: Mason Ruffner – guitar: Willie Green – drums: Cyril Neville – percussion

10.'Shooting Star'
Bob Dylan – vocal, guitar and harmonica: Daniel Lanois – omnichord: Brian Stoltz
– guitar: Tony Hall – bass: Willie Green – drums

Producer: Daniel Lanois
Engineers: Malcolm Burn, Mark Howard
Release Date: US: 22 September 1989, UK – 2 October 1989
Chart places – US: 30, UK: 6
Running time: 38:46
All songs written by Bob Dylan

It's a measure of Dylan's status that so many musicians who were artists
in their own right welcomed the chance to record with him. Texas-born
guitarist Mason Ruffner didn't have the name recognition of some of
the guests on *Knocked Out Loaded* or *Down in the Groove* (such as
Eric Clapton or Ron Wood), but his style was probably more in line
with Dylan's mood and mindset for *Oh Mercy*. Ruffner played on three
of the album's songs (not to mention several outtakes), including the
opening track 'Political World': the composition that kick-started Dylan's
songwriting after a fallow period.

He received help from another musician of note, with Farm Aid co-
founder John Mellencamp directing the song's music video – which
featured the singer performing in a banquet hall filled with moneyed
elites and their young female escorts. As is usual when Dylan wades
into political commentary, he avoids partisan identification and focuses
on the larger system. This explains his later comment that 'Political
World' reminded him of the *Empire Burlesque* song 'Clean Cut Kid.' The
observation that 'We're living in times where men commit crimes/And
crime don't have a face', is a symptom of the same moral malady afflicting
'Clean Cut Kid''s central figure, who 'bought the American dream but it
put him in debt.' Three decades later, 'Political World' still resonates, as

shown by soul singer Bettye Lavette's recording on *Things Have Changed*: her 2018 album of Dylan compositions.

While the sound of *Oh Mercy* is very different from the Traveling Wilburys album, both show Dylan approaching his material with confidence and conviction. The two projects briefly intersected when Dylan tried a version of the Wilburys song 'Congratulations' during a recording session with the iconic Louisiana musician Rockin' Dopsie. 'Congratulations' didn't make it to *Oh Mercy*, but the accordionist and his band helped Dylan articulate another ode to romantic entanglement.

The embrace of local culture notwithstanding, 'Where Teardops Fall' feels rooted in the Gershwin tradition. The lyrics, in particular, give it the atmosphere of a lost song from another era:

> We banged the drum slowly
> And played the fife lowly
> You know the song in my heart
> In the turning of twilight
> In the shadows of moonlight
> You can show me a new place to start

Like *Shot of Love* and *Infidels*, *Oh Mercy* finds Dylan ruminating on the end-times, but in more-measured terms than those earlier albums. 'Everything Is Broken' follows a similar path to 'Trouble' or 'License To Kill' in depicting a world gone wrong, but falls between those two poles lyrically; better crafted than the former, but lacking some of the latter's insight:

> Broken bodies, broken bones
> Broken voices on broken phones
> Take a deep breath, feel like you're chokin'
> Everything is broken

An alternate take, released on *The Bootleg Series Vol 8: Tell Tale Signs*, offers a glimpse of how the song developed in the studio. Along with a more direct arrangement, the *Bootleg Series* take includes some very different lyrics, giving the song a more individual dimension:

> I sent you roses once from a heart that was truly grieved
> Sent you roses someone else must have received

Dylan later mused that 'Critics usually didn't like a song like this coming out of me because it didn't seem to be autobiographical. Maybe not, but the stuff I write does come from an autobiographical place.' As a snapshot of his preoccupations, 'Everything Is Broken' fits well in the context of the album, and is delivered with conviction both vocally and instrumentally. This extended to the stage, where the song is one of Dylan's most frequently-performed from both *Oh Mercy* and the decade as a whole.

When in 1998 Sony Music released a promotional compilation of Dylan's work – to capitalize on the success of *Time Out of Mind* – his 1980s material was represented by 'The Groom's Still Waiting at the Altar,' 'Jokerman' and *Oh Mercy*'s 'Ring Them Bells'. If the two earlier songs represented the singer striving to translate spiritual concerns in a worldly context, 'Ring Them Bells' is a dispatch from a man who has cracked the code. Blending stately balladry and biblically-inspired lyrics, the song is a landmark that stands tall alongside Dylan's earlier statements of purpose:

Ring them bells for the chosen few
Who will judge the many when the game is through

Some commentators assert the supremacy of the alternate take featured on *Tell Tale Signs*. Questions of personal preference notwithstanding, this view seems just as indicative of fan contrarianism – that reflexively insists the alternate version of any post-1960s Dylan track must be superior to what he initially released – as it does the take's actual merits. Dylan hasn't played 'Ring Them Bells' in concert very often. But a live version from one of his now-legendary 1993 concerts at the Supper Club in New York City was also released on *Tell Tale Signs*. A multitude of cover versions further redress the balance, including recordings by Natasha Bedingfield, Gordon Lightfoot and Joan Osborne.

Osborne also recorded a version of *Oh Mercy*'s next song 'Man in the Long Black Coat,' which appeared on her 1995 debut album *Relish*. Reflecting on the production, Daniel Lanois told Clinton Heylin: 'It was quite fascinating to see the transformation that some of the songs made. They would begin as one story, and at the end of the night, they would be something else. One of my favorites is 'Man In The Long Black Coat,' which was written in the studio.'

Despite the song's in-the-moment origins and some judiciously-applied studio craft on the part of Lanois and his studio collaborator Malcolm

Burn, it has the aura of a song passed down through the ages. Dylan's carefully measured delivery gives this cautionary tale added impact:

Preacher was a talkin', there's a sermon he gave
He said, 'Every man's conscience is vile and depraved
You cannot depend on it to be your guide
When it's you who must keep it satisfied'

Oh Mercy's more-introspective second side begins with 'Most of the Time.' The atmospheric arrangement is arguably the album's finest example of Lanois finding an ideal accompaniment for the artist's internal dialogue, as they assure both themselves and the listener that they 'don't even remember what her lips felt like on mine'. The producer described his approach in a 2019 interview with journalist Chad Depasquale:

Most great art has contradiction in it, and that song certainly has that in its spine. I wanted to create a sonic representation of the contradiction. I wanted to have this little tormented orchestra, this little ensemble – playing cellos, violas and violins, but without cellos, violas and violins. So I used a Les Paul Junior cranked all the way up to 10, and I overdubbed four parts of this heavy single-note sound. So, the intertwining of these parts makes up that little exchange – that invisible string quartet that's immense from a distance. I wanted to make sure that the music was trying to destroy the singer at the same time as support him.

An alternate take released on *Tell Tale Signs* is interesting in its own right, but wouldn't have fit as well on the album. Accompanied only by his guitar and harmonica-playing, Dylan delivers the song with conviction. However, somewhat paradoxically, the stripped-down approach doesn't convey the sense of inner-dialogue like the album version manages to do – or even another version released on *The Bootleg Series*.

'What Good Am I?' continues the record's introspective thread. Reminiscent of 'Every Grain of Sand,' it draws from even earlier in *The Bible*. In chapter four of the 'Book of Genesis,' Cain replies to the Lord's question about the whereabouts of Abel – the brother he's just slain – with a question of his own: 'Am I my brother's keeper?' Caveats about reading too much autobiography into Dylan's work aside, this song suggests a belief on the singer's part that we *should* be our brothers' keepers:

> What good am I then to others and me
> If I've had every chance and yet still fail to see

Biblical allusions in Bob Dylan's work, started well before his born-again period, and have remained a powerful presence since. His effectiveness in integrating this aspect, ebbed and flowed throughout the 1980s, and while *Oh Mercy* provided an emphatic punctuation to this, the underlying thought never seemed too far out of mind during this time. In Bill Flanagan's book *Written In My Soul* – in discussing how a listener's familiarity with the *Bible* might impact their engagement with one of the songs from *Infidels* – Dylan said the following:

> The *Bible* runs through all US life, whether people know it or not ... It's the founding book ... the founding fathers' book anyway. People can't get away from it. You can't get away from it wherever you go. Those ideas were true then and they're true now. They're scriptural, spiritual laws. I guess people can read into that what they want. But if you're familiar with those concepts, they'll probably find enough of them in my stuff. Because I always get back to that.

Though the seven deadly sins aren't actually mentioned in the *Bible*, the critique of pride found in 'Disease Of Conceit' sounds rooted in those principles. In *Chronicles*, Dylan suggests the song may have been inspired by the 1988 scandal surrounding Jimmy Swaggart – an American televangelist who also happened to be the cousin of rock and roll pioneer Jerry Lee Lewis and country music star Mickey Gilley. When Swaggart's involvement with a prostitute came to light, the Assemblies of God church suspended him from preaching for three months. Swaggart rejected a further suspension, and resumed preaching, which led to the church defrocking him. If those events were the song's inspiration, it was written quite quickly, as Swaggart's initial public confession took place on 21 February 1989, shortly before the recording of *Oh Mercy* began. It's quite likely Dylan had other examples of pride-before-the-fall in mind for this *de facto* companion piece to 1979's 'Gotta Serve Somebody.' Where that earlier song admonishes listeners to be mindful of a higher power, 'Disease of Conceit' speaks to the consequences of not following that advice:

> Give ya delusions of grandeur
> And a evil eye

Give you the idea that
You're too good to die
Then they bury you from your head to your feet
From the disease of conceit

Like many of Dylan's best songs, 'What Was It You Wanted' invites multiple interpretations, but also renders making distinctions between them slightly beside the point. Regardless of whether the song is directed at his audience or one of the women in his persistently-tangled personal life, the combination of stark lyrics and a simmering groove – punctuated by his harmonica-playing – makes the same impact.

Whatever you wanted
What could it be
Did somebody tell you
That you could get it from me

'Shooting Star' – the album's final track and another song written in the studio – can likewise be viewed through multiple lenses. A mix of reverie and reminiscence, the simple, striking image at its heart, allows the singer to seamlessly unite earthly and heavenly concerns:

Seen a shooting star tonight
And I thought of you
You were trying to break into another world
A world I never knew

The song's gentle melody and soul-searching lyric made it Dylan's strongest album-closer since *Infidels*. He thought enough of the song to make it one of only two recent compositions featured in his 1994 *MTV Unplugged* performance – an outtake from *Oh Mercy* being the other.

Leaving off stronger songs than some that made the album-cut, was nothing new for Dylan, especially in the 1980s. Neither were the assertions that by putting aside songs such as 'Caribbean Wind' or 'Blind Willie McTell,' the singer had somehow eviscerated the album. What differentiated *Oh Mercy* from *Shot of Love* or *Infidels*, was a sense that while songs such as 'Dignity' or 'Series Of Dreams' might've added to the record's luster, their absence didn't intrinsically make it a lesser album. Lanois recalled, 'I did say that I didn't think that certain songs belong on the record. He took it fine, but he bucked me on a few of those decisions.' For *Oh Mercy*, Dylan seemed to view disagreements about song choices or how songs were recorded, as a feature rather than a flaw:

In the end, there always has to be some compromise of personal interests, and there was, but the record satisfied my purposes and his. I can't say if it's the record either of us wanted. Human dynamics plays too big a part, and getting what you want isn't always the most important thing in life anyway.

One of the songs Lanois felt strongest about including – 'Series of Dreams' – was also the first of those to be released officially, as the final track of the initial *Bootleg Series* set. Though not quite as perfect an encapsulation of Dylan's artistry as *Biograph*, the 1991 set distinguishes itself by giving concrete evidence that Dylan had more to offer than nostalgia: a point the impressionistic song emphasized. 'Series Of Dreams' didn't chart when released as a single, but nevertheless was included in 1994 on his third *Greatest Hits* collection. The approach of well-known songs mixed with other highlights was generally consistent with the two previous volumes. However, the fact that much of the potential audience probably already owned many of the songs on other albums, made it one of the least essential Dylan collections. The obvious exception was a revamped version of 'Dignity,' which retained only Dylan's contribution from the *Oh Mercy* sessions. Producer Brendan O'Brien – best-known for his work on albums by Pearl Jam and Stone Temple Pilots – replaced Lanois and the New Orleans musicians with an effective but less-distinctive backing track. O'Brien also helped deliver a superior rendition of the song when he joined Dylan's band on keyboards for the 1994 *MTV Unplugged* performances.

Two versions of 'Dignity' released on *Tell Tale Signs* offer further snapshots of its evolution. In addition to a full-band take featuring Mason Ruffner and the others, the set also includes a demo where Dylan accompanies himself on piano. Both reflect the multiple approaches he and Lanois pursued – none of which quite satisfied either man – as well as the singer's lyric refinements. Though the rewriting process involved sacrificing a sly reference to George Bernard Shaw's 'Don Juan In Hell,' and imagery like 'Death is standing in the doorway of life,' Dylan deserves kudos for sacrificing individual moments for the sake of the overall song.

Two other songs from the *Oh Mercy* sessions show that the willingness to rework rather than abandon songs that emerged in Dylan's 1980s work, carried through to the next decade. Both 'God Knows' and 'Born In Time' appeared on his 1990 album *Under the Red Sky* in very different versions than those released on *Tell Tale Signs*. Rather than the impromptu assembly of *Oh Mercy* musicians, the *Under the Red Sky* recordings featured higher-profile guests like David Crosby and star guitarists Jimmie and Stevie Ray Vaughn. The end results were good in their own right, but Dylan himself seemed less engaged there than in the earlier takes.

For the moment, though, Bob Dylan had reestablished his artistic – and to some extent commercial – credibility, and had done so largely on his own terms. *Oh Mercy* appeared on the best-of-the-year lists of various publications, such as the British magazine *Q*, and *The Village Voice*. *Rolling Stone* also included it in their list of the 100 best albums of the decade. Sandwiched between albums by Sonic Youth and Bruce Springsteen, its placement at number 44 was Dylan's only appearance on the list (his contributions to The Traveling Wilburys and Artists United Against Apartheid notwithstanding). The *Rolling Stone* writer encapsulated the consensus opinion that, 'While it would be unfair to compare *Oh Mercy* to Dylan's landmark Sixties recordings, it sits well alongside his impressive body of work.'

On the personal front, Dylan became a grandfather in November 1989 when his daughter Maria Himmelman had a daughter. Meanwhile, his association with Chabad Lubavitch continued when he performed again at their annual telethon, singing 'Hava Nagila' along with his son-in-law Peter Himmelman and actor Harry Dean Stanton. The event was an apt punctuation mark for a decade in which questions about Dylan's religious beliefs were far more plentiful than answers.

Epilogue: Before They Close the Door

More than three decades since the release of *Oh Mercy*, Bob Dylan's 1980s songs have been recorded by a multitude of artists – a possibility that would've seemed unthinkable at the time. Even allowing for the general proliferation of tribute albums since the late-1980s, the attention his songbook receives is remarkable. It also speaks to the profound increase in his status since then.

Dylan might not have envisioned *Oh Mercy* as more than just a solid collection of songs, but in retrospect, the album occupies an eminent place in his broader body of work. While none of its songs are as transcendent as 'Jokerman' or 'Every Grain of Sand' (though 'Ring Them Bells' comes close), their overall quality fully justified Bruce Springsteen's praise of Dylan's current work at the Rock and Roll Hall of Fame induction. Dylan may only have sought to 'secure the place where (he) was at,' but delivering his first album in over a decade for which no equivocation seemed necessary gave him time to find a path 'to climb the next mountain.'

But it wouldn't be a clear path for him. 1990's *Under the Red Sky* included some very good songs – including several originally written for *Oh Mercy* – but was poorly received in comparison to its predecessor. Dylan took a very different direction for his next two records. *Good As I Been To You* and *World Gone Wrong* both spotlighted the older music that had influenced him – mixing traditional folk and blues songs with compositions by songwriters such as Stephen Foster and Blind Willie McTell. Though neither release sold especially well, both received good reviews, and in 1994, *World Gone Wrong* won Dylan his second competitive Grammy award for Best Traditional Folk Album.

The following year's *MTV Unplugged* release resulted in further Grammy nominations, and sold better than the pair of solo recordings that preceded it, but also seemed like another exercise in securing his position, as opposed to a step forward. When the step forward came two years later, it proved to be a cross between a leap and a marathon. A major health scare in mid-1997 might've added somewhat to public curiosity about his next album, but it was the new songs – recorded with Daniel Lanois well before the 56-year-old singer went into hospital – that made it so successful. Released in September, *Time Out of Mind* was the first solo Dylan album to reach the US Top 10 since *Slow Train Coming*.

With just nine studio albums released in the intervening 24 years since 1997, Dylan's studio work has adopted a very different cadence than in the 1980s when he released nearly an album a year. It would be tempting to attribute this merely to a renewed emphasis on quality over quantity, but such a flippant assessment ignores the fact that records such as *Love and Theft* and *Modern Times* are filled with unique songs every bit as confident as the 1989 album that returned Dylan to prominence. The same applies to apparent detours like 2009's *Christmas In the Heart* or any of the three collections of standards released between his two most recent albums of original compositions: *Tempest* and *Rough and Rowdy Ways*. These records all embody Dylan's apparent resolution of the tension between his standing as an original artist in his own right and one of the foremost purveyors of a long-standing musical tradition. This has happened in tandem with a recognition that his relationship with the audience is different from that of many artists of similar status. Shortly after the release of *Time Out of Mind*, Dylan told Robert Hilburn:

> I don't have any one kind of fan or follower of this kind of music, like say, U2 or Bruce or any of these young groups today who consistently keep their followers because what they are doing is variations of the same things ... I didn't come out of the same environment. My tradition is older than all that. I came out of the environment of folk music.

Whether he recognizes it or not, Dylan is also a tradition unto himself, and other artists continue to interpret his work at a rate that calls to mind the 1960s heyday when The Byrds and other groups regularly recorded his songs.

One of the principal moments came in October 1992 with a Madison Square Garden concert celebrating Dylan's 30 years as a recording artist. In addition to the expected mix of rock artists, the concert – jokingly referred to as Bobfest – showcased his songwriting versatility through performances by The Clancy Brothers, Stevie Wonder and various members of the Carter/Cash family, among others. As good as the performances were, the event became more relevant for its intersection with a cultural flashpoint and a song that wasn't performed as a result. On 3 October 1992, Irish singer Sinead O'Connor sparked controversy when she tore up a picture of Pope John Paul II during a *Saturday Night Live* performance protesting the sexual abuse of children within the Catholic Church. Because mainstream awareness of the problem was still low, many perceived her action as an attack on the popular pontiff and the Church itself, and the uproar drowned out her message. The anger carried through to 16 October when she took the stage at the Dylan concert to an onslaught of booing. After a defiant rendition of 'War' – the Bob Marley song she performed before the photograph incident two weeks earlier – a visibly shaken O'Connor left the stage without singing Dylan's 'I Believe In You.'

The segment of the New York audience that drove O'Connor away, probably felt satisfaction in the moment, but all they really accomplished was to deprive themselves of what would've been an excellent performance. A recording of her rehearsal of 'I Believe In You' was later released as a bonus track when the concert album was reissued in 2014, two years after the release of another Dylan tribute from O'Connor. In 2012 she recorded *Shot of Love*'s 'Property of Jesus' for *Chimes of Freedom*: a collection benefiting Amnesty International. With 75 songs from artists ranging from Angelique Kidjo and the Kronos Quartet to Diana Krall and Jackson Browne, *Chimes of Freedom* offers an even more expansive view on Dylan's songwriting.

Many of the artists who contributed to the 2012 set had recorded Dylan songs before and have since, including Bryan Ferry and soul singer Bettye LaVette, who have both recorded full albums devoted to Dylan's work. While Ferry's *Dylanesque* sidestepped the two decades between 'Simple Twist of Fate' and 'Make You Feel My Love,' LaVette's *Things Have Changed* took the inverse approach, with nearly half of the songs being from Dylan's 1980s albums. *Standing in the Doorway* – a collection of Dylan songs released by Chrissie Hynde on the eve of his 80th birthday in May 2021 – also drew heavily on his 1980s work.

Another sign of how Bob Dylan's work from the 1980s is being reevaluated came in 2017 with the London premiere of the stage musical *Girl From the North Country*, directed and with a book by Irish-born playwright Conor McPherson. Of the two-dozen Dylan songs the show uses to help tell its story – set in the American Midwest during the Great Depression – four come from *Infidels* and *Empire Burlesque* (with an instrumental version of 'Blind Willie McTell' for good measure) plus two songs from *Saved* added for the show's Broadway run. In the liner notes for the Broadway cast recording, McPherson acknowledged the mixed reputation of the singer's 1980s work and the controversy the 'born again' period sparked while conveying how compelling he found those recordings personally.

Listening to these 40 albums, I found myself pulled into this area of his music again and again; albums like *Slow Train Coming*, *Saved* and *Infidels*, struck by the passion and intensity of his writing at this time. Whatever this search was, wherever it had been leading him, it had certainly yielded artistic treasure.

Girl From the North Country soon transferred to the West End and made its American debut at New York's famed Public Theater in late-2018. The Broadway production initially opened in March of 2020 just a week before the COVID-19 pandemic shut down theaters in New York. In an interview for the New York Times, Dylan described how moving he found the show, which reopened in October of 2021. Perhaps the most telling comment about it – and by extension Dylan's overall body of work – came in a July 2017 review in British newspaper *The Observer*. Theatre critic Susannah Clapp wrote, 'I came away feeling that Dylan has been writing not a series of songs but an unfolding chronicle.'

Like *Girl From the North Country*, the *Bootleg Series* releases continue to provide an alternative vantage point for that chronicle. The 16th volume in the series, *Springtime in New York*, was the first to focus exclusively on the 1980s. Covering the years 1980 to 1985, the September 2021 release complements *Trouble No More* by presenting additional material from the recording sessions for *Shot Of Love* along with rehearsals for his 1980 'musical retrospective' tour.

The former largely reaffirms the judgments about the song choices for *Shot Of Love* sparked by previous archival releases, which covered the album's more noteworthy outtakes, though, 'Yes Sir, No Sir' stands out as one of Dylan's more guitar-heavy tracks from this period. Aside from a variety of covers, one of the more interesting pieces is an alternate mix of the song 'Lenny Bruce'. The richer instrumentation on the track offers a glimpse of what *Shot Of Love* might have sounded like had Dylan agreed to let producer Chuck Plotkin polish the recordings a bit.

Covers are also a big part of the tour rehearsals. The mix of traditional gospel songs like 'Jesus Met the Woman at the Well', the r&b classic 'Fever' and contemporary pop songs such as Neil Diamond's 'Sweet Caroline' and the 1979 soft-rock hit 'This Night Won't Last Forever' anticipated the balance of spiritual and secular on *Shot Of Love*.

The remainder of the set was devoted to material from the recording of *Infidels* and *Empire Burlesque*. The former is more interesting, not because any of the previously unreleased songs invite rethinking *Infidels*' track-list but rather for the window into Dylan's creative process that the recordings offer. The two different takes of 'Don't Fall Apart on Me Tonight' show that though the song was fully formed, the singer needed time to work out the right sound for it. Likewise, multiple tracks from the set trace how 'Too Late' evolved into 'Foot of Pride'. Even recordings that were substantially similar to those on Infidels offered compelling alternate lyrics, such as 'You're a king among nations / You're a stranger at home' from an earlier iteration of 'Jokerman.'

The songs from *Empire Burlesque* are presented in a more stripped down form than the original release. While this was a major focus of pre-release publicity, the end results weren't so much revelations as reflections of a different aesthetic. Adding synthesizers and other studio enhancements didn't fundamentally change the songs, and neither does removing those elements. The alternate versions of 'Emotionally Yours' or 'Seeing The Real You At Last' might be more to some fans' tastes than the album versions, but the underlying quality of the songs stands apart from their production.

Tom Petty and the Heartbreakers keyboardist Benmont Tench, who most recently worked with Dylan on *Rough and Rowdy Ways*, offered a thoughtful assessment of Empire Burlesque's sound in the liner notes for Springtime in New York. 'Bob has to get a record feeling the way he wants, and all I can think of is: that's the way he wanted it to feel,' said Tench who also noted that, 'A song is a living entity to him – and maybe that was just where it was living that day.' As Bob Dylan resumes live performances, Tench's comment seems especially relevant, not just to his work in the 1980s but also the whole of his musical career.

Also available from Sonicbond ...

On Track series

Tori Amos – Lisa Torem 978-1-78952-142-9
Asia – Peter Braidis 978-1-78952-099-6
Barclay James Harvest – Keith and Monica Domone 978-1-78952-067-5
The Beatles – Andrew Wild 978-1-78952-009-5
The Beatles Solo 1969-1980 – Andrew Wild 978-1-78952-030-9
Blue Oyster Cult – Jacob Holm-Lupo 978-1-78952-007-1
Marc Bolan and T.Rex – Peter Gallagher 978-1-78952-124-5
Kate Bush – Bill Thomas 978-1-78952-097-2
Camel – Hamish Kuzminski 978-1-78952-040-8
Caravan – Andy Boot 978-1-78952-127-6
Cardiacs – Eric Benac 978-1-78952-131-3
Eric Clapton Solo – Andrew Wild 978-1-78952-141-2
The Clash – Nick Assirati 978-1-78952-077-4
Crosby, Stills and Nash – Andrew Wild 978-1-78952-039-2
The Damned – Morgan Brown 978-1-78952-136-8
Deep Purple and Rainbow 1968-79 – Steve Pilkington 978-1-78952-002-6
Dire Straits – Andrew Wild 978-1-78952-044-6
The Doors – Tony Thompson 978-1-78952-137-5
Dream Theater – Jordan Blum 978-1-78952-050-7
Elvis Costello and The Attractions – Georg Purvis 978-1-78952-129-0
Emerson Lake and Palmer – Mike Goode 978-1-78952-000-2
Fairport Convention – Kevan Furbank 978-1-78952-051-4
Peter Gabriel – Graeme Scarfe 978-1-78952-138-2
Genesis – Stuart MacFarlane 978-1-78952-005-7
Gentle Giant – Gary Steel 978-1-78952-058-3
Gong – Kevan Furbank 978-1-78952-082-8
Hawkwind – Duncan Harris 978-1-78952-052-1
Roy Harper – Opher Goodwin 978-1-78952-130-6
Iron Maiden – Steve Pilkington 978-1-78952-061-3
Jefferson Airplane – Richard Butterworth 978-1-78952-143-6
Jethro Tull – Jordan Blum 978-1-78952-016-3
Elton John in the 1970s – Peter Kearns 978-1-78952-034-7
The Incredible String Band – Tim Moon 978-1-78952-107-8
Iron Maiden – Steve Pilkington 978-1-78952-061-3
Judas Priest – John Tucker 978-1-78952-018-7
Kansas – Kevin Cummings 978-1-78952-057-6
Led Zeppelin – Steve Pilkington 978-1-78952-151-1
Level 42 – Matt Philips 978-1-78952-102-3
Aimee Mann – Jez Rowden 978-1-78952-036-1
Joni Mitchell – Peter Kearns 978-1-78952-081-1
The Moody Blues – Geoffrey Feakes 978-1-78952-042-2
Mike Oldfield – Ryan Yard 978-1-78952-060-6
Tom Petty – Richard James 978-1-78952-128-3
Porcupine Tree – Nick Holmes 978-1-78952-144-3
Queen – Andrew Wild 978-1-78952-003-3
Radiohead – William Allen 978-1-78952-149-8
Renaissance – David Detmer 978-1-78952-062-0

Also available from Sonicbond ...

The Rolling Stones 1963-80 – Steve Pilkington 978-1-78952-017-0
The Smiths and Morrissey – Tommy Gunnarsson 978-1-78952-140-5
Steely Dan – Jez Rowden 978-1-78952-043-9
Steve Hackett – Geoffrey Feakes 978-1-78952-098-9
Thin Lizzy – Graeme Stroud 978-1-78952-064-4
Toto – Jacob Holm-Lupo 978-1-78952-019-4
U2 – Eoghan Lyng 978-1-78952-078-1
UFO – Richard James 978-1-78952-073-6
The Who – Geoffrey Feakes 978-1-78952-076-7
Roy Wood and the Move – James R Turner 978-1-78952-008-8
Van Der Graaf Generator – Dan Coffey 978-1-78952-031-6
Yes – Stephen Lambe 978-1-78952-001-9
Frank Zappa 1966 to 1979 – Eric Benac 978-1-78952-033-0
10CC – Peter Kearns 978-1-78952-054-5

Decades Series
The Bee Gees in the 1960s – Andrew Mon Hughes et al 978-1-78952-148-1
Alice Cooper in the 1970s – Chris Sutton 978-1-78952-104-7
Curved Air in the 1970s – Laura Shenton 978-1-78952-069-9
Fleetwood Mac in the 1970s – Andrew Wild 978-1-78952-105-4
Focus in the 1970s – Stephen Lambe 978-1-78952-079-8
Genesis in the 1970s – Bill Thomas 978178952-146-7
Marillion in the 1980s – Nathaniel Webb 978-1-78952-065-1
Pink Floyd In The 1970s – Georg Purvis 978-1-78952-072-9
The Sweet in the 1970s – Darren Johnson 978-1-78952-139-9
Uriah Heep in the 1970s – Steve Pilkington 978-1-78952-103-0
Yes in the 1980s – Stephen Lambe with David Watkinson 978-1-78952-125-2

On Screen series
Carry On… – Stephen Lambe 978-1-78952-004-0
David Cronenberg – Patrick Chapman 978-1-78952-071-2
Doctor Who: The David Tennant Years – Jamie Hailstone 978-1-78952-066-8
Monty Python – Steve Pilkington 978-1-78952-047-7
Seinfeld Seasons 1 to 5 – Stephen Lambe 978-1-78952-012-5

Other Books
Babysitting A Band On The Rocks – G.D. Praetorius 978-1-78952-106-1
Derek Taylor: For Your Radioactive Children – Andrew Darlington 978-1-78952-038-5
Iggy and The Stooges On Stage 1967-1974 – Per Nilsen 978-1-78952-101-6
Jon Anderson and the Warriors – the road to Yes – David Watkinson 978-1-78952-059-0
Nu Metal: A Definitive Guide – Matt Karpe 978-1-78952-063-7
Tommy Bolin: In and Out of Deep Purple – Laura Shenton 978-1-78952-070-5
Maximum Darkness – Deke Leonard 978-1-78952-048-4
Maybe I Should've Stayed In Bed – Deke Leonard 978-1-78952-053-8
Psychedelic Rock in 1967 – Kevan Furbank 978-1-78952-155-9
The Twang Dynasty – Deke Leonard 978-1-78952-049-1

and many more to come!

Would you like to write for Sonicbond Publishing?

At Sonicbond Publishing we are always on the look-out for authors, particularly for our two main series:

On Track. Mixing fact with in depth analysis, the On Track series examines the work of a particular musical artist or group. All genres are considered from easy listening and jazz to 60s soul to 90s pop, via rock and metal.

On Screen. This series looks at the world of film and television. Subjects considered include directors, actors and writers, as well as entire television and film series. As with the On Track series, we balance fact with analysis.

While professional writing experience would, of course, be an advantage the most important qualification is to have real enthusiasm and knowledge of your subject. First-time authors are welcomed, but the ability to write well in English is essential.

Sonicbond Publishing has distribution throughout Europe and North America, and all books are also published in E-book form. Authors will be paid a royalty based on sales of their book.

Further details are available from www.sonicbondpublishing.co.uk. To contact us, complete the contact form there or email info@sonicbondpublishing.co.uk